The New Evangelization
2003-2013 Missionary Letters

ASH Production
KC • Washington DC

The New Evangelization 2003-2013 Missionary Letters
1st edition - November 2013 | 2nd edition - December 2015
Collected letters of *A Simple House of Sts. Francis and Alphonsus*
Edited by Clark Massey.

Published in the United States of America by
S&T Minuteman Press for ASH Productions.

All rights reserved. No part of this book may be used or reproduced without written permission.
For information please contact:
A Simple House, PO Box 31259, Washington DC 20030
Phone 202-678-5898

Manufactured in the United States of America

ISBN: **978-0-615-88541-4**

A Simple House of Sts. Francis and Alphonsus is a lay missionary apostolate serving the poorest neighborhoods of Washington, DC, and Kansas City, MO. All Simple House work is done by full-time and part-time volunteers.

Introduction
by

**Donald Cardinal Wuerl
Archbishop of Washington**

for

**The New Evangelization
2003-2013 Missionary Letters**

The Church exists in order to evangelize. This is to say that the church is missionary in nature. Anyone who reads through the Acts of the Apostles sees that as witnesses to the Resurrection and our salvation in and through Christ, the apostles were called to be missionaries, carrying this Good News out to the World. As Pope Benedict XVI writes in *Deus Caritas Est*, "The Church's deepest nature is expressed in her three-fold responsibility: of proclaiming the word of God (*kerygma-martyria*), celebrating the sacraments (*leitourgia*), and exercising the ministry of charity (*diakonia*). These duties presuppose each other and are inseparable." For the Church, charity is not a kind of welfare activity which could equally well be left to others, but is a part of her nature, an indispensable expression of her very being (*Deus Caritas Est*, 25).

The ministry of charity is essential to the evangelizing mission of the Church. Charity has always been a hallmark of the Christian way of life. The universal Church and our local church make a tremendous impact for the good in and through its charitable works. In response to the call for a New Evangelization, our charitable organizations are asked to guard against separating people's material needs from their spiritual needs. In some cases organizations and individual volunteers have grown hesitant to speak the name of Jesus in the course of their work or extend an invitation to "come and see" the life of a local parish. All of the Church's charitable works seek to attend to both the material and spiritual needs of the people we serve.

It is a pleasure for me to introduce the beautiful ministry of A Simple House through *Missionary Letters from the New Evangelization*. These letters share with you the experience of "friendship evangelization" as practiced by the members and volunteers of the community. At A Simple House, invitation is the foundation of its ministry. Clark Massey, founder of A Simple House, describes the first day of their outreach in May of 2004 through the lens of the New Evangelization. "Nine individuals met...to pray and reach out for the first time to the Chesapeake neighborhood. 400 Easter bags were prepared full of candy, small toys, religious items, and information. Our plan was to invite people to Church, make sure everyone was able to celebrate Easter, and form contacts which would become the foundation of our ministry" (Letter, May 2004). Invitation to encounter the Risen Christ is the mission of A Simple House.

The first moment of any evangelization originates not from a program, but in an encounter with a person, Jesus Christ, the Son of God. The Church maintains that "it is the same Lord Jesus who, present in his Church, goes before the world of evangelizers, accompanies it, follows it, and makes their labors bear fruit" (Doctrinal Note: Some Aspects of Evangelization, December 2007).

Friendship evangelization is a relationship of mutual sharing. Volunteers not only bring the love of Christ to others, they encounter Christ in the people they befriend. Members of A Simple House write beautifully of their own ongoing conversion. For Catholic evangelization is marked by the realization that all of us continually grow in our love of the Lord. In these letters you will read how prayer and reflection on Scripture not only prepare members of the community for ministry, it is Scripture and prayer that help them reflect more profoundly on their experiences. One member who came to A Simple House to learn how Christ fits into serving the poor discovered "we cannot recruit Christ into our ideology. We need to be converted to Christ." In this Christ becomes the source from which we live.

    I am grateful for the publication of these letters at this time in which our Holy Father, Pope Francis, is teaching us about the link between evangelization and solidarity. Pope Francis counsels "to those in possession of greater resources, to public authorities and to all people of good will who are working for social justice: never tire of working for a more just world, marked by greater solidarity! ...The culture of selfishness and individualism that often prevails in our society is not what builds up and leads to a more habitable world: it is the culture of solidarity that does so, seeing others not as rivals or statistics, but brothers and sisters" (Address to the Community of *Varginha, July 25, 2013).*

    In sharing their experience of friendship evangelization, the members of A Simple House invite us to consider how our acts of charity are both acts of evangelization and expressions of solidarity.

Donald Cardinal Wuerl
August 1, 2013

TABLE OF CONTENTS

Introduction *by Donald Cardinal Wuerl*	5
Prologue	10
Founding Letter	13
The First Outreach	20
Friendship Evangelization	26
Spiritual Poverty	30
Love	34
Four Brothers	37
Providence	42
House of the Three Teresas	46
Ugly Things	51
The Two Ways	55
Charity in Truth	58
Generosity of the Poor	63
Life *by Jess*	67
Old Testament World	69
Conversion	72
Family Support *by Laura*	75
Voluntary Poverty *by Ryan*	79
Prosperity	83
Jarrell's Death *by Ryan*	86
Roaches *by Ryan F.*	90
Fixing Problems *by Jess*	94
Forgiveness *by Kelly*	96
Going Out West	99
Gentleness and Letting Go *by Laura*	103
Beauty Will Save the World	108
Leaving DC	111
Fasting *by Laura*	114
George's Story	116
George's Story, Part 2	118
Rachel's Story *by Danielle*	121
The Jacksons' Very Bad Day	124
Difficult Ministry *by Laura*	128

New Evangelization	132
God and Fun *by Ryan*	136
The Hidden Poor	139
Rachel's Story, Part 2 *by Danielle*	142
Patricia's Blizzard *by Bianca*	146
Ryan and Laura's Wedding	149
Easter Stories *by Laura*	153
Solidarity *by Mary*	157
Networking	161
A Turtle and a Chicken *by Ryan*	165
The Woodsman	169
Mark's Story *by Liz*	173
Victims or Losers	176
Pit Bulls and Thanksgiving Turkeys *by Ryan*	179
Grace Abounds *by Bianca*	183

PROLOGUE

Pope John Paul II and Pope Benedict XVI have called for a New Evangelization. This is often misinterpreted as new energy and new technology used for the old evangelization. The New Evangelization needs new energy and technology, but fundamentally, it is a new approach to witness and dialogue. Since the Council of Trent, evangelization has been caught in an intellectual and apologetic mode. This mode compares and contrasts different beliefs, and it stresses orthodoxy in faith. The New Evangelization needs to be a full evangelization. Right thinking (orthodoxy) needs to be married with right practice (orthopraxis) for the new life promised by the gospel to ignite.

> To evangelize means: to show this path—to teach the art of living. At the beginning of his public life Jesus says: I have come to evangelize the poor (Luke 4:18); this means: I have the response to your fundamental question; I will show you the path of life, the path toward happiness—rather: I am that path.
>
> The deepest poverty is the inability of joy, the tediousness of a life considered absurd and contradictory. This poverty is widespread today, in very different forms in the materially rich as well as the poor countries. The inability of joy presupposes and produces the inability to love, produces jealously, avarice—all defects that devastate the life of individuals and of the world.
> This is why we are in need of a new evangelization—if the art of living remains an

unknown, nothing else works. But this art is not the object of a science—this art can only be communicated by one who has life—he who is the Gospel personified.[1]

The New Evangelization needs to demonstrate a new way to live. This new way of life is not a set of strictures and rules for goody-goodies. It is not an intellectual argument against anything. It is not even a defense of something. It is a position for Christ, and it is a conquering force of love, forgiveness, and freedom. It is good news.

Mother Teresa was a groundbreaker for the New Evangelization. She witnessed with and without words, and the world was able to hear her witness. Pope John Paul II also demonstrated the New Evangelization when he reinvigorated sexual morality. His Theology of the Body took a set of "don'ts" and transformed them into a discussion of beauty, virtue, and freedom. Both of these saints were creative in how they reinvigorated evangelization. They made new life more accessible to the modern world, and their methods gave freedom for the Holy Spirit to operate.

Before A Simple House, I was an economist. My old coworkers and classmates have been a blessing to me and to this work. In early 2003, I left that job in order to follow God into this work, but the result of the work was never certain. I felt so compelled to start A Simple House that even failure would have been a welcome relief.

Since 2003, six seminaries have assigned seminarians to work with A Simple House. There have also been over twenty-five people received into the Church and over twenty-five people have served as full-

---

[1] Joseph Cardinal Ratzinger, "The New Evangelization: Building the Civilization of Love" (Address to catechists and religion teachers on the Jubilee of Catechists, December 12, 2000).

time missionaries with A Simple House. In some ways, the fruits of the work make it look like a success, but it rarely feels like a success. This book contains the reflections experienced during the work.

These letters were sent to the friends, family, and sponsors of Simple House missionaries. The letters were meant to give an accurate sense of poverty, life, and evangelization. They contain stories that show the many sides of poverty and the interesting people grappling with these issues. The stories also try to show missionaries accepting the complex task of loving and serving the poor.[2]

After sharing these reflections, some people understand the ministry of A Simple House at an intuitive level. They "get it" and see it as simple Christian charity and evangelization. Others find it troubling. It is troubling because it is not scientific social work or proselytizing. It is an experiment and a basic response to the universal call to holiness. Everyone is called to bring the personal love of God to people, and this work is one response to that call. This response is, at the core, the New Evangelization.

Clark Massey

---

[2] Some redundant material and local news has been removed from the letters.

FOUNDING LETTER

Dear Friends and Family,   November 17, 2003

    I quit my job, sold my motorcycle, and poured my life savings into the founding of a small charity in Southeast Washington, DC. The charity is called "A Simple House of Sts. Francis and Alphonsus." It is an opportunity to more fully live my Christian faith and to minister to God's poor in a direct way.

    God has been very generous. Besides startup money, He has provided an extra refrigerator, a used minivan, and a very supportive community of friends. The charity will run on a shoestring budget with hope, faith, and many prayers in the gas tank.

    In the short term, we need money to buy our first location and home base. We have chosen a small home in Southeast DC. The price of the house is $55,000 with a closing in mid-December. <u>Every donation over a single digit is very significant.</u>

    The neighborhood to be served is South Congress Heights, also known as Chesapeake. It's a neighborhood most people are afraid to drive through. Buildings have been boarded up and burned out, the remains of cars line the sides of roads, and public areas are littered with garbage. Later in the day and throughout the night, prostitution, drug dealing, and gun shots are common. All of these factors coexist in the neighborhood that is raising more children than any other neighborhood in DC.

The school system serving the Chesapeake neighborhood has completely failed. Sixty-five percent of students at the local high school are illiterate. Many youth and adults are solely dependent upon a spoken witness to the Gospels.

Fortunately, it's not as bad as it seems from afar. God has abandoned no one in this life, and there are things to build on even in the worst situations. Many grandparents are lovingly providing for their grandchildren, mothers are trying to learn to be better parents, and there are even criers of the Gospel message. We hope to take this cry to the next level and make it an intimate cry to one person at a time.

The charity of A Simple House is focused on befriending the poor. Volunteers from the house will help clean homes, distribute groceries, and pray with the poor.

To set the tone of the ministry, a few hours of house cleaning will be offered as a gift. Cleaning homes is an important part of the ministry because it makes volunteers servants of the poor and it's a great way to find out the other interests and needs of the people being served. There are elderly and disabled individuals who really need help with cleaning, and some children are suffering in unsanitary conditions due to the neglect of their parents. In addition, it shows a sincerity which will hopefully remain in friendships and prayerful relationships. Needless to say, cleaning is an inexpensive ministry, and there may not be enough funds for anything else.

Other physical needs met by the House may include a basketball, a game for a child with a disability, a cake on a birthday, or food for a hungry family. We might be able to provide more meals if we just dropped off bags of generic groceries, but we hope to touch more hearts by giving in a personal way. A friend of mine is an African American priest who has served in some of the rougher neighborhoods of DC. In one of his homilies he mentioned the good ol' days: "Remember when people used to bring you food when you were sick or grieving, and they brought it on their fine china!" The success of this charity will not be measured by the number of meals given or homes cleaned. It will be measured in the sharing of faith, hope, and love. We hope to treat people as individuals and serve them as neighbors and friends.

There is no desire to be a "total" ministry which would get someone off drugs, their kids to school, food in the cupboards, and a new job. We simply aim to rekindle hope through little stages of help and friendship. Chesapeake is an environment dominated by violence, sexual promiscuity, child abandonment, and many other sins. A few healthy prayerful moments can make a large difference when there is every temptation to despair.

Many people have looked perplexed when I've tried to explain the goal of A Simple House because the goal is not fully charitable or fully ministerial. The charity seems inefficient because it's ministerial, and the ministry seems inefficient because it is charitable. Yet charity and ministry have a natural marriage springing from love. In a wonderful way, St. Francis and Mother Teresa made this marriage work.

St. Francis of Assisi left his elevated state in society and went to personally clean the wounds of lepers. St. Francis could have raised money or worked to create benefits for the lepers. Instead he felt called to touch them, love them, and be their intimate neighbor using his own finger to remove the decaying flesh from their wounds.

Mother Teresa had a similar mission. She would not use the donations she received to build sewer systems, dig wells, or otherwise address the structural problems that led to many of the diseases she was treating. Although she was in favor of public works, that was not her mission. Her mission was to bring to the dying the love of Jesus Christ, a love that is superior to any other love, in a personal way.

Although both of these saints may confuse the world with their inefficiency, they brought many thousands to love Christ in their own lifetimes and established more hospitals, orphanages, schools, and houses of charity than any purely charitable organization. In the case of St. Francis, the Franciscan brothers are still cleaning the wounds of lepers 800 years later.

A Simple House is to be a place where there is no real distinction between work and life. There is not a "going home" at the end of the day. No distinction will be made between food for the poor and food for volunteers. The house will be in a poor neighborhood and similar to the houses the poor live in. In a true sense, there will be a living with the poor.

The house is a special home base from which to distribute groceries to the poor, provide housing for volunteers, and reach out in a personal, Christian way as friends of the poor. In the future, it may also be an ideal place for a neighborhood Bible study.

In the last year, two experiences shifted my life away from my career in economics and towards a life with the poor of DC. For over a year, I've been volunteering at a Catholic Worker house in Northwest DC, and for the last nine months, I've been living in the house. The homeless of DC have been dining, showering, doing laundry, and exchanging clothes in my home. During open house, I'm the dedicated table server and dishwasher. Afterwards, I wash the extremely dirty laundry. It's not unusual to wash a load three times with hot water and triple the recommended level of detergent. I've also been living with five gentlemen who are in transition from homelessness. For me, it's been a transition also, and I'm very thankful to John and Maria Owen for the opportunity to serve God through my neighbors. The Owens and the deceased Michael Kirwan are special inspirations of A Simple House.

Another instructor by witness and example is the long time DC missionary Mary Lyman Jackson. I've been working (and will continue working) with her group of missionaries going door to door and providing youth Bible study in a project neighborhood of Northeast DC. These ministries have given me many ideas about "what is possible" when working with the poor, and have shown me how many friendly friendship-starved people there actually are.

The motto of A Simple House is to promote a wonderful and radical falling on the cross of Jesus Christ for grace and support. A radical fall on the cross of Christ is an obvious fall. Thus, we strive to follow the instruction, "Freely you received, freely give. Do not acquire gold, or silver, or copper for your money belts, or a bag for your journey, or even two coats, or sandals, or a staff; for the worker is worthy of his support" (Mt 10:7–10). If this House succeeds, it will be the obvious work of God's providence. We do not receive support from the government, a church community, or private endowment. If the House is doing the honest work of Christ, funds will be there to support it. If not, we are not honest, or Christ wants us to move on. Thus, all money donated will be spent in the following couple of months, and from our current financial outlook, it may be spent the day it arrives.

Our only source of financial support is individual donors. The cost of the home is $55,000, and the entire amount must be paid on the settlement date. Bank financing is unavailable for a fixer-up house, and I'm appealing to you for short-term and long-term help.

In the short-term, money is needed to pay for the house and start up the ministry, and in the long-term (may God provide a long-term), funds are needed to support the evangelical and charitable work of the ministry. No money of the ministry is paid out in the form of salaries, no volunteer is financially profiting from the ministry, all donations are tax exempt under section 501(c)(3) of the I.R.C., and if the ministry is forced to fold, all property and funds go to a ministry with similar goals and purposes.

It's my hope that people with a similar vision and motivation may join the work of A Simple House of Sts. Francis and Alphonsus as live-in volunteers, but as for now, there is only one live-in volunteer and a wonderful community of supportive friends. Please pray for our success.

Sincerely,

Clark Massey

Statistics about the Chesapeake Neighborhood

- There are over 30,000 people living in the Chesapeake neighborhood, and 98.7% of Chesapeake's population is from a racial minority.

- There are over 7,000 families in Chesapeake, and 70.1% of the families in Chesapeake, the highest of any neighborhood in DC, are led by single mothers.

- Chesapeake has more children as a fraction of the population and more people per household than any other neighborhood in DC.

- The police precinct that patrols Chesapeake investigates more homicides than any other precinct in the city.

- According to the Washington Post, September 4, 2003, the illiteracy rate at Chesapeake's high school is 65.1%.

THE FIRST OUTREACH

Dear Friends and Family,   May 2004

    We obtained a small 125-year-old house in Southeast Washington, DC, on the last day of 2003! It was the cheapest house sold in the District that didn't need to be demolished. The house is attached on one side with two bedrooms, one bathroom, a large basement, and termite damage. My parents gift-leased the house and donated the renovation supplies sight unseen. Lawrence Kirwan, the brother of Michael Kirwan, has been extremely generous with his talents and time.[3] He spent six days a week for three months working on the repairs. Because of the generous way we received and repaired our first home, most of the founding donations have been saved for direct ministry.

    God has also provided the ministry with many amazing friends and courageous volunteers. Their actions have shown a great commitment to our purpose, and I thank God for all his blessings despite my faults. My friend Chuck Beck moved into the house from the start and will be helping out for a few more months.

    I would also like to thank the individuals and families who donated in response to my last letter (especially my former coworkers). Each donation was a personal encouragement and grace for me. Thank you for building my faith and making this ministry a reality.

---

[3] Michael Kirwan was a famous Catholic Worker in Washington, DC. He passed away in 1999.

The Work

On the Saturday morning before Easter, nine individuals met at A Simple House to pray and reach out for the first time to the Chesapeake neighborhood. 400 Easter bags were prepared full of candy, small toys, religious items, and information. Our plan was to invite people to Church, make sure everyone was able to celebrate Easter, and form contacts which would become the foundation of our ministry.

I had been praying that the gentlemen who congregate outside the apartment complex would be asleep, but as we arrived, they were already outside and business had begun. When offered Easter bags, the gentlemen declined and enthusiastically helped volunteers find the apartments with children. In God's typical fashion, He converted what I saw as a problem into a blessing.

We are still trying to develop relationships with the mothers and grandmothers of the neighborhood. This outreach will grow more slowly, but God keeps things moving fast enough that our heads seem to be constantly underwater. If everything went as quickly as I would like, it would be a gigantic mess.

In addition to the Chesapeake neighborhood, our immediate neighbors in Anacostia have begun to find us, and various individuals from around the city who need our help stumble upon us.

The Charism

We feel most called to serve mothers and grandmothers who struggle to get by with violence, promiscuity, drugs, and prostitution threatening to usurp their family. Helping children and men is a natural extension of helping mothers. There are situations where children are not allowed to leave the house due to the crime outside, neglected children are being taken in or fed by neighbors, and six children sleep without mattresses in a single bedroom. The women who raise children and reach out to others in this near impossible atmosphere are the real ministers. It is our job to support them and keep them well supplied. We do this by getting to know individual families and meeting their unique needs. These needs may include food, help with bills, home repairs, or cleaning. We try to do all this in the spirit of friendship, and we believe that our presence and support is as important as the physical assistance we provide.

A complete charitable act should have three parts which please God: the sacrifice, the caring and appreciative interaction of rich and poor, and the actual tangible alleviation of suffering. Modern charity and government programs often fail to capture even two of these three aspects. They can be obligatory, faceless, and received with a sense of entitlement. Sometimes they do not even alleviate physical suffering.

A Simple House of Sts. Francis and Alphonsus is only a small Christian charity, but it has the opportunity to capture all three of these aspects in a beautiful way. We are a ministry without professional counselors, social workers, fund-raising officers, etc. We are only volunteers trying to live the universal calling to Christian charity. Sometimes a professional is necessary, but only a Christian is needed most of the time. The people we serve are not clients. They are our friends and neighbors created in the image of God.

It is our goal to create opportunities for fruitful ministry and reach people that institutional charities are failing. Please pray that we will have the resources and graces necessary to keep this goal alive.

> At the moment of our death, you and I, whoever we might have been and wherever we have lived, Christians and non-Christians alike,

every human being who has been created by the loving hand of God in His own image, shall stand in His presence and be judged according to what we have been for the poor, what we have done for them. Here a beautiful standard for judgment presents itself. We have to become increasingly aware that the poor are the hope of humanity, for we will be judged by how we have treated the poor. We will have to face this reality when we are summoned before the throne of God: "I was hungry. I was naked. I was homeless. And whatever you did to the least of my brethren, you did it to me."

-Bl. Teresa of Calcutta

A Deeper Look at the Situation

The sidewalk in front of A Simple House is host to women walking the streets, men selling drugs, and children walking to and from school. While parking in front of the house, I've had a woman try to get into my car and men try to sell me their wares. Behind our home, stolen cars are abandoned and stripped while children play in their backyard and watch. The Chesapeake neighborhood is in worse shape than ours. It is a place where

- there is enough food but children go hungry because of neglect,
- cars are stolen not for profit but for fun,
- people understand that drugs ruin lives but they use them anyway,
- women are prostituting themselves without pimps or physical coercion.

This is also a place with few missionaries and many children. This is spiritual poverty.

Despite these problems, the inner city also has a special spiritual wealth. Many people concede that God controls the big things like hurricanes, earthquakes, life, and death, but the disadvantaged have a special appreciation of Jesus in the small things like favorite foods, coincidences, and little breaths of fresh air. We hope to celebrate the spiritual wealth and address the spiritual problems through our ministry.

We wish to embrace the good even in the morally muddled and difficult situations, which are plentiful. Through all of the pain of a complicated moral problem, we should realize that babies are good, and it's okay to celebrate their arrival despite the moral implications of the situation. This does not condone the situation but concedes the goodness of babies! Children should be welcomed to the world with joy, not frowns and scowls.

A Simple House is not trying to slow pitch or water down the Catholic truth. Truth is plain, simple, and beautiful, and it is our challenge to express it this way. The good news of Jesus Christ is that God has a tender, particular, and intimate love for us, and He wants us to enter into this relationship with Him. Morality and styles of devotion are effective only after this initial good news has been preached with joy. We hope to show this joy in the help and friendship we freely give.

Our Plans

In the upcoming months, we plan to launch two projects. The first will allow families to donate cribs, baby carriages, and baby supplies to the poor through us, and the second will be a Bible study/adult literacy program called, "Learn to Read while Reading the Word." Both of these programs will help us further develop relationships with the neighborhood and individual families.

In the long term, please pray that volunteers will respond to God's call to help women suffering from prostitution, and that God will allow us to open a house run by women for women. Explicit and non-explicit prostitution is common in Southeast DC. In the explicit cases, drugs may be driving the problem, but there are many ways that sex and relationships can be treated as a commodity. These non-explicit forms of prostitution also need to be healed.

I cannot properly express my gratitude to all the individuals and families who contributed through us to the spiritually and materially poor of Washington, DC. It is a great honor to work for you. Prayers, donations, and volunteers are still needed for the work, and it is your generosity of heart, self, and property that make the will of God more active in the world. Thank you. You are in our prayers.

Praise be to God.

Clark Massey

> It seems to me that this great poverty of suffering in the West is much harder to solve. When I pick up some starving person off the street and offer him a bowl of rice or a piece of bread, I can satisfy his hunger. But a person that has been beaten or feels unwanted or unloved or fearful or rejected by society experiences a kind of poverty that is much more painful and deep. The cure is much more difficult to find.
> -Bl. Teresa of Calcutta

FRIENDSHIP EVANGELIZATION

Dear Friends and Family,   August 2004

    Through the grace of God and generous donations of time and money, A Simple House is providing an authentic Christian witness to thirty-five families. I am humbled by the way the Lord has blessed our charitable work with encouragement and marvels. Since our last letter, the ministry has formed a network of close friendships with our neighbors in the Chesapeake neighborhood.

The Work
    Delivering food and baby supplies, driving people to church, thwarting evictions, conducting home Bible study, and prayer are the backbone of our ministry. All of our volunteers' time has been consumed by these most basic forms of evangelization and ministry.
    Ms. Johnson lives with her ten children in a small townhouse. The children slept on slats, and there was not always enough food in her pantry. The greatest physical need of the family was more space, but because of holes in the walls from mice and humans, she could not pass an inspection to transfer her family into a larger home. A Simple House helped Ms. Johnson repair her home, buy mattresses, feed her children, and go to God in prayer. These acts of kindness were made possible by our donors and volunteers, and we have built a relationship with Ms. Johnson such that she remembers the name of every volunteer she has ever met (all seven of them).

Our ministry involves an intimate meeting with families in their own homes. The Bible study and prayer that results is personal and genuine. In fact we have had so many requests to visit church as our guests that there have not been enough vehicles to oblige everyone.

On August 21st, A Simple House is hosting its first barbeque in the Chesapeake neighborhood. We are planning to pitch a gigantic tent and serve hotdogs and hamburgers to the 168 families and approximately 650 children of the Chesapeake neighborhood. Many children in the neighborhood do not eat regularly. We hope to feed them and help with school supplies for the coming year. The parishioners of St. Thomas More in Washington, DC, have also pledged their support to create an atmosphere of Christian fellowship and friendship at the barbeque.

The Problem

When we see material worshiped through greed, might worshiped through violence, or sex worshiped through lust, we must unmask the true Lord through acts of love. Even those caught up in violence, greed, and lust cannot pretend that they will reach fulfillment through these means. They have an inherited knowledge that these are dead ends, but they fail to grasp the greatness, goodness, beauty, and majesty of God who is our End. This is spiritual poverty.

The corridors of Chesapeake Street and Southern Avenue are heavy drug-trafficking areas. As in all drug markets, the vices of lust, violence, and greed thrive. These vices create competition and obstacles between people and God.

We are bringing a difficult message of transformation in Christ. We must have faith in the conversion of ourselves and others as the avenue of change.

> I will sprinkle clean water upon you to cleanse you from all your impurities, and from all your idols I will cleanse you. I will give you a new heart and place a new spirit within you, taking from your bodies your stony hearts and giving you natural hearts. I will put my spirit within you and make you live by my statutes careful to observe my decrees. You shall live in the land I gave your fathers; you shall be my people, and I will be your God. (Ez 36:25–28)

Conversion is possible to everyone and comes from God via prayer.

Our Method

Friendship evangelization is the method we use to spread the Gospel. People should be caught up "by the catching force—the sympathetic influence of what we do, the evident fullness of the love our hearts bear to God!" (John Henry Cardinal Newman)

We try to relate to others no matter who they are. By embracing life's deepest meanings, Christians opt out of the generally accepted world for the deepest realities. If we do not come across as real, we are deceiving ourselves and not truly sympathizing with our brothers. People should understand us, and after meeting a Christian, people should say, "I know that man."

People need good example, encouragement, and sometimes a word of correction. All of these are ways to instruct people in the word of God. Encouragement and good example are often the more difficult way to witness to the Word of God. The poor usually have enough people giving them disapproval and very few people giving them encouragement or a good example. This is what we are doing.

Conclusion

    The idea that the survival of A Simple House is completely dependent upon the generosity of individual donors and volunteers boggles some. It's as if they think government grants are necessary for charity. This "surprise" is part of our Christian witness.

    We have a very tight budget with no employees and very little overhead. Thank you for supporting this ministry through prayer, time, and money. I will continue to work to ensure that every gift you make has an impact, and I hope we will be able to expand our reach and start new projects through the further generosity of volunteers and donors.

Thank you, and may God bless you.

Clark Massey

SPIRITUAL POVERTY

Dear Friends and Family,   December 2004

Since the last newsletter, there have been four daylight shootings in the Chesapeake neighborhood. Two of the shootings were fatal, and two resulted in serious injuries. Some apartments have been riddled with bullets, and children have witnessed the violence. In response, the police have increased their presence and converted a vacant apartment into a holding cell. A few of the apartment buildings have been declared public nuisances.

Unwed mothers and grandmothers are the vast majority of the neighborhood's tenants. The healthiest families survive from check to check, and if unemployment or mismanagement causes the lights or heat to be turned off, the mother carries a large psychological and physical burden. By getting to know people and visiting their homes each week, we spread the Gospel while learning where help is most needed and what help is most appropriate. Your generosity is what lifts the burden off people's backs, and the Good News is what sets their spirits free.

The Good News is that God loves you in a particular and intimate way. He doesn't love you just because you are human or part of His creation; He loves you individually and particularly. He doesn't love you from afar; He holds you in the palm of His hand (Is 49:15–16) and embraces you in the depths of your soul. He even likes you.

Spiritual desolation is the greatest poverty, and that is what we are trying to address. I've seen Christ work an amazing transformation in a woman through the love, prayers, and generosity of our volunteers. When we met her, she was contemplating suicide, intending to abort her unborn child, and her five children were without heat. She had gone through many trials in her childhood and adult life, and her depression was disabling. She had been prescribed many drugs and met with many psychologists, but they could not address her feeling of being unloved and wronged by God.

Her conversion to Christ has been so beautiful that the adjective miraculous is insufficient. The love of God struck her as an amazing surprise and a life-changing event. We delivered a few bags of groceries once a month, and read the Bible with her every Friday. We did not offer anything more except our friendship and faith. As time passed she decided to keep her unborn baby. She made pilgrimages with us to some churches in DC and attended church on Sunday. God has transformed her life. Her entire family has a beautiful humility and sweetness about them. She has registered her children for school vouchers, and we are helping them to relocate to a healthier neighborhood. These are the amazing fruits of spiritual work.

There is a temptation to become engrossed in the idea of a political solution to the problems of the inner city. The study of social welfare, welfare economics, and sociology all focus on the political aspect of the problems. Every political solution is fundamentally a material solution, but materials do not seem to be lacking in the inner city of Washington, DC.

Jobs, treatment for addiction, and food are available, but it's as if something mysterious stands in the way. The poor have experienced a great loss of hope which leads to self-defeating behavior. It has been called "a situation that defies a solution." The real problem, however, is a spiritual problem, and to provide material goods without friendship or spiritual support only continues the problem.

When someone loses hope, they lose interest in their own welfare and their family's future, which causes behaviors resembling a slow suicide. We need to convince them to live! This is a hard job, and we are trying to reach some of the hardest cases. When we bring friendship and God, we are bringing love and spiritual food. Friendship with another is almost a prerequisite of conversion, and many people are hungry for this friendship.

Amazing blessings have been poured upon the ministry since the last newsletter. Two families gave large financial donations, a family donated a large number of coats and organized a neighborhood coat drive, a family in Texas donated a Lincoln Towncar, Visitation High School has helped us stock the food pantry and visit the poor, and there have been many other sorely needed donations. In addition, Copley Crypt Church and some individuals have made regular monthly donations. Thank you to everyone who makes our work possible!

This Christmas, we are trying to reach people as individuals. One room of our house has been converted into The Christmas Room! The Christmas room is for holding, hiding, and wrapping Christmas presents. We hope to stuff it to the gills. With your help, A Simple House has already provided Christmas gifts for 98 children by buying toys and clothes which match their unique interests and needs. If there were more funds, we could make Christmas memorable for at least 50 more children.

To reach mothers, grandmothers, and families, A Simple House is creating Christmas baskets which will each include a ten pound ham, a box of chocolates, fruit, and an individual religious gift depending upon what we know of the family. The gifts will include wall crucifixes, framed pictures, Bibles, puzzles, and even a few movies. We are planning to deliver 100 baskets.

The immediate fruit of these outreaches is joy on Christmas Day. The larger (less seen) fruit is the lasting love and friendship it creates in a neighborhood plagued by violence. This is the most important fruit of our work, which is so hard to describe and measure.

As stated in the first newsletter, "If this house succeeds, it will be the obvious work of God's providence." Your generosity is our budget, and we apply all donations to the immediate work at hand. All donations are tax exempt under section 501(c)(3) of the Internal Revenue Code.

Help and holiness are the two greatest needs. Holiness is the prerequisite for efficiently or effectively serving Christ. Please pray that we will receive more help and holiness in the coming year.

May God bless you.

Clark Massey

LOVE

Dear Friends and Family,   April 2005

    The Saturday before Easter, A Simple House reached its one year anniversary of active ministry. On the anniversary, volunteers delivered Easter bags full of goodies, toys, and religious articles to the children of the Chesapeake neighborhood and chocolate with invitations to church for the grownups. The outreach was a complete success. Since the last newsletter we also delivered approximately 100 Christmas baskets and angeled personalized Christmas gifts for approximately 100 children.
    During the first year, A Simple House has addressed the spiritual and material dimensions of poverty by delivering groceries, assisting mothers with infants, leading in-home Bible studies, and helping people pray. The ministry has also been flexible enough to meet unique needs such as thwarting evictions and making sure families have heat. General outreaches have been used to start relationships and evangelize. In addition to the Easter bags, Christmas baskets, and angeling Christmas toys, first-year general outreaches included a neighborhood barbeque, coat drive and distribution, school supply drive and distribution, and an appeal to help pregnant women and new mothers. Thank you for making all of this possible.

    Our witness is having the desired effect. Love is being returned as fast as we try to give it away. Two sisters spent nine hours preparing a soul-food banquet for some of our volunteers. This loving gift was large enough to stuff twenty-five people. Many other people we serve want to help out in some way, but we have not discovered enough ways to harness their energy. Besides the charitable and prayerful response, one of our friends was received into the Church on the vigil of Easter. With an impressive amount of study and prayer, this person made the decision to give herself to Christ. We celebrated the event with a big midnight party.

I am constantly astonished by the miraculous way God heals. We serve families and individuals who have survived multiple events which would have been enough to shatter an average person. It is amazing to see people who have been through heinous crimes become psychologically, emotionally, and spiritually healthier than people who have been sheltered and granted many privileges. God heals.

William Barclay pointed out, "We will never change men from the outside. New houses, new conditions, better material things only change the surface. It is the task of Christianity to make, not new things, but new men." Many programs have tried using material things, productivity, accomplishment, and education to make someone realize their dignity, meaning, happiness, or fulfillment. Unfortunately, all of these approaches have failed to achieve even one of these ends.

The only approach remaining is Love. "God," wrote Lacordaire, "has willed that no good should be done to man except by loving him, and that insensibility should be forever incapable either of giving him light, or inspiring him to virtue."

When it is not clear how to apply love to a problem, it is useful to reflect on the words of Mother Teresa: "Jesus is the unwanted to be wanted. Jesus is the beggar to give him a smile. Jesus is the drunkard to listen to Him. Jesus is the drug addict to befriend Him. Jesus is the prostitute to remove from danger and befriend her. Jesus is the prisoner to be visited. Jesus is the old to be served. To me: Jesus is my God."

    Our Lord really has nothing better to do than bless us. He cannot run out of miraculous blessings, and He can't get tired while giving them away. On the final day, God will not say, "I would have blessed you more, but I'm too cheap." Nor will He say, "I would have blessed you more, but my infinite self was too busy (keeping all the subatomic particles in existence)." Nor will He say, "I would have blessed you more, but I really don't like miracles." God will say, "I am so in love with you, I showered you with every blessing you could possibly hold." We need to ready ourselves to recognize and receive His blessings. Just as our sin brought suffering into the world, our weakness frustrates the redemption.

    There is a great material and spiritual need in the inner city. This need is a call to Christians for Christianity.

Sincerely,

Clark Massey

FOUR BROTHERS

Dear Friends and Family,   July 2005

Within the neighborhood we serve, there are four brothers who have raised themselves. They are now high school and college age and live in an apartment without a parent, guardian, or electricity. Their apartment has become a center for drug use and a hangout for neighborhood boys. The brothers have lost close friends to street violence, and they receive more attention from the police than from any other organization.

Although most people have written them off as a "neighborhood problem," these brothers have embraced every interaction with A Simple House. They have facilitated us helping their mother who suffers from drug abuse, and when we arrive unannounced, they organize their friends into a circle for prayer. Our interactions with them have been shot through with grace, and there is a crying need for more witnesses to Christ in their lives.

The four brothers' neighborhood, which is the community A Simple House primarily serves, will probably be condemned in the next twelve months. Families are moving away, and numerous buildings in the complex have been declared public nuisances because of crime. In one particular building, fifteen out of sixteen apartments were occupied one year ago. Today, only four apartments are occupied, and one is being used by the police.

Leaking roofs have caused apartment ceilings to cave in, and the property owners are not making the necessary repairs. In addition, the owners have not fulfilled their contractual obligations to replace carpets, repaint units, or fight mold. We believe the owners are squeezing money from government housing vouchers (Section 8) until the properties are condemned or deserted to make way for gentrified housing.

This corruption is victimizing people who do not have the resources or time to fight back. Families must catch up on bills before the government will allow them to transfer their housing vouchers, and even the families who took good care of their units do not expect to have their security deposits returned.

Your generosity has helped families with bills, security deposits, visits to new places, cleaning supplies, and food for the week of the move. Sometimes a little assistance has helped a family move into a house rather than an apartment or into a healthy neighborhood.

As a result of this exodus, we visit a spider web of people throughout the city while continuing to serve the community left behind. When the apartment complex finally closes, we will choose another neighborhood to serve close to our home. There is no shortage of ministerial opportunities in this area.

Many of the mothers we serve also want to volunteer. In response to their requests, A Simple House organized two lasagna cooking days. After volunteering for a whole day in the small Simple House kitchen making as many as eighteen lasagnas, the mothers come with us to deliver the lasagnas to other needy families, and of course, everyone leaves with a lasagna for their own family.

These days are beautiful in many ways. They allow opportunities for spiritual discussion, they feed many people, they allow the poor to be generous, and they are fun. This generous fun is significant evidence of evangelization working.

Our letter of August 2004 described the situation of Ms. Johnson and her ten children. By repairing her home, we helped Ms. Johnson transfer within the projects to a six-bedroom house. Your generosity provided the children of the family with mattresses and helped her rent a truck for the move. Over the last year, we have visited and prayed with Ms. Johnson and her family over a dozen times, and she remembered the name of every volunteer she ever met (all seven of them).

Ms. Johnson moved to her new home in January of 2005, and in May, she died. We talked with her the day of her death to schedule a home visit for the following morning. That night, she suddenly succumbed to a heart condition. Volunteers visited the home the next day and prayed with the traumatized family and friends. During this hard time, volunteers cooked for the family, bought diapers for the youngest children, took the oldest children grocery shopping, and much more. A Simple House also assisted in paying for Ms. Johnson's funeral which was delayed for almost a month due to insufficient funds. At the funeral, it became clear that Simple House volunteers were the primary Christian witnesses in Ms. Johnson's life. Thank you for making this work possible.

The stories of the brothers, the lasagna days, and Ms. Johnson are examples of how Christians can instigate righteousness. Jesus described our role in the Kingdom of God as leaven, salt, and flame (Lk 13:21; Mt 5:13–16). Leaven, salt, and flame transform things, and it only takes a small amount of any of them to create a profound change. A little leaven creates most of the volume of the bread. A little salt flavors an entire meal, and the flame of a candle lights an entire room. We should never be discouraged because we are small and simple. Christ wills to raise, flavor, and light the world using us as humble instruments, and for our part, we must constantly challenge and reorient ourselves to follow His call.

When we act in this way, the Kingdom grows like the mustard seed (Mk 4:26–33), and the Kingdom is filled with righteousness, peace and joy (Rom 14:17). A Simple House is dedicated to helping Christ transform people, which is the only true way to transform society. "I never think in terms of crowds in general but in terms of persons. Were I to think about crowds, I would never begin anything. It is the person that matters. I believe in person-to-person encounters" (Bl. Teresa of Calcutta).

Fr. Adam Ryan, a monk of Conception Abbey, arrived at A Simple House on his birthday. That morning Simple House volunteers drove a new mother to the hospital. Fr. Adam's 50th birthday corresponded to the 0th birthday of a new baby girl, and they spent quality time celebrating the occasion together. At the end of his visit, A Simple House hosted a dinner and evening of recollection. Seventeen people attended the event, and Fr. Adam's preaching renewed their amazement at the Word of God.

In June, Jim Hardcastle joined me as a full-time volunteer in our house in Southeast Washington. Jim had been managing Olsson's Books in Old Town Alexandria and using his free time to work with the homeless. Jim's radical gift of time and energy is a great relief and should significantly increase the number of people served by the ministry. When commitment such as his is combined with the generosity of many individual donors like you, a great work is done one person at a time.

Please pray for everyone served by A Simple House, and please say a special prayer for the children of

Ms. Johnson as their lives continue to be turned upside down.

Thank you, and may Christ continue to fill our cups faster than we can pour them out.

Clark Massey

PROVIDENCE

Dear Friends and Family,   September 2005

    Two weeks ago, I walked into the bank to find only $350 in our account. In one hand I had bills totaling over $350 and, in my other hand, I had a stack of donations. God has never fallen short on providing, although sometimes He is just in time. It is our goal to continue living on God's providence in an obvious way and never hoard the gifts He gives us. This philosophy keeps us praying and ensures that your generosity is always used to its full potential.

    For over a year, your generosity has made possible our work with Ms. Wilson and her four children. When we met Ms. Wilson, she lived in an apartment without heat and was on her way to being evicted. Due to mixed up paperwork, she was not receiving her medication. She had lost over a hundred pounds, her glands and eyes were swollen, and with some excuse, she was continually in a sour mood. On the day of her eviction, she called A Simple House to ask for help saving her most important possessions. In the next few months, we helped Ms. Wilson move between the homes of relatives and various shelters, and did many small things to help her obtain health care and stay encouraged. During those trying months, Ms. Wilson's daughter became pregnant and her son was wounded in a drive-by shooting. In a Bible study with the family, we read the story of Jesus' birth. We chose the reading as a scriptural platform to introduce the faith without realizing that Ms. Wilson's daughter was sixteen, homeless, unmarried, and due on Christmas day. The Holy Spirit enjoys coincidences, and He speaks to the poor in powerful ways.

Today, Ms. Wilson is staying in a nice temporary apartment, her health is much better, and she is preparing to become a grandmother. She is even getting glasses to help with her eyesight. Last week, Ms. Wilson gave us a gift and a letter that read, "My family is very grateful to have you as a friend. You have been with me and my family through thick and thin and I want you to know that we all love you."

The hardest part of sharing our faith is presenting morality in an attractive way. Paul states, "The fruit of the Spirit is love, joy, peace, patience, kindness, goodness, faithfulness, gentleness and self-control. Against such things there is no law" (Gal 5:22–23). We must speak of morality in the light of these fruits without characterizing it as the "bad news" of Christ. As John Paul II put it, "God, who alone is good, knows perfectly what is good for man, and by virtue of his very love proposes this good to man in the commandments." Morality is part of the Good News, and by teaching morality we teach the path to our greatest happiness.

God's will can be summed up as "be good," and translated into human terms this means "be supernaturally good and holy." Christianity is not about being mostly good and at least respectable. Christians are called to imitate Christ, and this involves offering our entire life as a gift. This gift is to the poor, our families, our church, our neighbors, our spouses, and God. F.R. Maltby said, "Jesus promised His disciples three things—that they would be completely fearless, absurdly happy and in constant trouble." If twice the number of people woke up every morning and tried with their whole being to live Christ, the world would be a radically different place. This may sound like a utopian dream, but what God wills He also provides the grace to accomplish.

We need to be careful of an attitude that can creep into our thinking and masquerade as love. The attitude is a tendency to degrade someone with pity and low expectations. This attitude is in our religion when we meet a sinner who seems to us too far gone to convert or be reborn in Christ, and it is in our politics as a strange racism which is not hate but patronizing kindness.

Many people (especially inner-city adults) are being written off as incapable of reform and conversion, and society tries to placate the problems of the inner city with expensive social programs. As a dogma, we believe that the grace is available to everyone for conversion, and we also know that God is never cheap with His gifts. We need to address these problems with Christian charity, prayer, and evangelization.

True Christian charity (which includes respect) is the best way to spread the love of God.

> Men take glory in resisting those who try to impose anything on them by force; they make it a point of honor to raise countless objections against the wisdom that aims at arguing everybody, all the time, around to its own point of view. But because there is no humiliation involved in allowing oneself to be disarmed by kindness, men are quite willing to yield to the attraction of its advances.
>
> -Dom Jean-Baptiste Chautard, O.C.S.O.

During the summer, A Simple House gave out copies of Roald Dahl's Charlie and the Chocolate Factory to encourage reading. If a neighborhood child finished the book and passed a quiz, they won Wonka candy, tickets, and a ride to the movie for themselves and their mother. We hope to do something similar for C.S. Lewis's The Lion, the Witch and the Wardrobe. In addition,

Visitation High School assisted in preparing school supply bags for 115 children of the families we serve.

Three good friends of A Simple House are moving on. This September, our great coworker, Katherine Hamm, joins the Franciscan Sisters of the Renewal in the Bronx. Katherine and the Christian Service Club of Visitation High School have helped with our food pantry, Christmas outreach, and home visits. In October, board member Glynnis LaGarde will enter a Dominican convent in Lufkin, TX. Glynnis has been with A Simple House since its inception and has participated in many home visits, Bible studies, and general outreaches. (She even helped renovate the house.) In addition, our first chairman of the board, Laura Cartagena, has moved abroad. Please pray for their continuing work for Christ.

This November, we will enter a new neighborhood with a Thanksgiving outreach while continuing to serve our old neighborhood. Please pray that we will develop many sincere friendships and raise adequate funds for the outreach. Br. Peter, a Carmelite seminarian from Vietnam, Br. Francis, a Redemptorist seminarian from New York City, and Kathleen Looney, the new Christian service coordinator of Visitation High School, will be working with us this year and assisting in these enterprises. In addition, we look forward to the fresh input of Luis and Margarita Cartagena (parents of Laura Cartagena) at our board meetings. Luis Cartagena will take over as our new chairman.

May God's peace be with you.

Clark Massey

HOUSE OF THE THREE TERESAS

Dear Friends and Family, November 2005

We need to give and expect a very high degree of love and not settle for anything less. By searching in this way, we come to God. Somehow we innately know that our inner secrets, our body, and our love should not be sold for any price because they are valuable beyond price. But we are told to confess our inner secrets to each other (Jas 5:16) and to give all of these things in marriage for free (1 Cor 7:2-5). When we give what is priceless for nothing, we are God-like.

The world describes someone as God-like if they seem to be all-powerful, all-knowing, or have physical perfection. Christianity turns this idea on its head. The defining attributes of God are His immeasurable generosity, complete forgiveness, and total love. God created us in His image and likeness, and after the fall, we are relearning to be God-like. God inspires and reinforces this journey.

Niccolò Machiavelli declared the world's logic when he said, "There is nothing so self-defeating as generosity, for the more generous you are, the less you are able to be generous." The Christian knows that there is nothing that requires more practice than generosity. If we are ever to be greatly generous, we must first be a little generous. To be God-like is to let our finite charity approach His infinite charity, and our finite resources will miraculously approach His infinite resources.

Pursuing charity requires faith, and faith is a necessary ingredient in all miracles. Miracles likewise reinforce and strengthen our faith. We must be aware, however, that sin also has a reinforcing factor. Sometimes it is called a darkening of the intellect, addiction, or habit. With every sin, we have more reason to escape God, and this desire to escape is behind the reinforcing spiral of sin. If we choose to sin for self-exaltation, our situation will be lower and sinful self-exaltation will be more tempting when we finish. If we sin to escape from despair, the situation will be more desperate when we return. Problems get worse when we escape from them.

Our challenge is to reach out and help others break from the road of sin, and become established on the road to God. We do this by sharing our relationship with Christ. All true Christian missionary activity is merely this: introducing Christ to our neighbors and helping them enter into a transforming relationship with Christ. This transformation involves good works, and the mark of true knowledge about God is good works (Mt 7:15–27). The inverse is also true. Good works can school us in knowledge about God. Love is only an idea until it is applied. It would be shameful to arrive at heaven with only a theoretical love and not a living love.

The Real Big News

We are opening a new house! The new house will be called A Simple House of Sts. Teresa, Therese, and Teresa (the House of the Three Teresas for short), and it is located in the Shaw neighborhood of Washington, DC. The house was founded by Michael Kirwan as a Catholic Worker shelter for homeless women and has been run by Connie Ridge and the Kirwan family. We thank God and the Kirwan family for this remarkable gift and opportunity. We will be moving into the house this January, and we hope to use the house as a home for female volunteers and temporary missionaries. Please pray that God will send us the right volunteers and that He will bless all of us with the necessary sanctity and grace for His work. Please also pray for the new projects this house will make possible.

      God's ways are making headway with a group of individuals that we did not expect to focus on, seventeen- to twenty-year-old males. Some young men have been coming to church with us, and they show a sincere interest in discussing the basic questions of life. They are coming from an environment full of drugs, shootings, sexual exploitation, broken families, and unfinished educations. This environment usually leads young men to prison. Please pray that all of them will become saints! We need them, and they need God. This is an exciting new area of the ministry, and Fr. Pope of St. Thomas More Parish has suggested that we start an evening meeting for people who are coming directly from the streets. At the meeting we would discuss the good news, morality, and God in a flexible but direct format depending upon the needs of those attending. Please pray for this endeavor.

      On September 30, twenty people gathered in the small Simple House kitchen to hear William Gorman of the Archdiocese of Washington speak on evangelization. Given that we have had only two speakers, we don't pay them, neither of them have Nobel prizes, and both of them have wowed their audience, this has been the best speaker series ever, and we have decided to call it "The Best Speaker Series Ever." The next speaker in the series will be Fr. Charles Pope on Friday, March 24. We hope to have the event at the House of the 3 Teresas. Everyone is invited, and dinner will be provided.

Thank you for making this ministry possible.

Clark Massey

Who are the Three Teresas?

St. Teresa of Avila (1515-1582) — lived during a time of corruption and drew people back to God by her books and her foundations of nuns and priests. Her writings discussed prayer and the spiritual life in a comfortable, familiar, and approachable way. She inspired many people to pray with renewed vigor. She is one of the 33 doctors of the Church.

St. Therese of Lisieux (named for St. Teresa of Avila) (1873-1897) — entered a convent at the age of 15 and died of tuberculosis at the age of 24. Her one book is a spiritual autobiography entitled *The Story of a Soul*. Her simple outlook dignified the smallest tasks with eternal significance and came to be called the "little way." She is one of the 33 doctors of the Church.

Blessed Teresa of Calcutta (named for St. Therese of Lisieux) (1910-1997) — reawakened and gave credibility to the idea of radical Christian discipleship in a world that had grown cynical and unimaginative. She is best known for her lively faith and her care of the poorest of the poor.

Mental prayer consists of what was explained: being aware and knowing that we are speaking, with whom we are speaking, and who we ourselves are who dare to speak so much with so great a lord. To think about this and other similar things, of how little we have served Him and how much we are obliged to serve Him, is mental prayer. Don't think it amounts to some other kind of gibberish, and don't let the name frighten you.

-St. Teresa of Avila

The most trivial work, the least action, when inspired by love, is often of greater merit than the most outstanding achievement. It is not on their face value that God judges our deeds even when they bear the stamp of apparent holiness, but solely on the measure of love we put into them. . . And there is no one who can object that He is incapable of even this much, for such love is within the reach of all men.

-St. Therese of Lisieux

I am not sure exactly what heaven will be like, but I do know that when we die and it comes time for God to judge us, He will not ask, "How many good things have you done in your life?" He will ask, "How much love did you put into what you did?"

-Bl. Teresa of Calcutta

UGLY THINGS

Dear Friends and Family,   Easter 2006

    Since the last letter many ugly things have happened. Two of the mothers we serve attempted suicide; one overdosed on pills, and the other cut her throat. Another mother was near-fatally stabbed in the head and back. Two families we minister to have been devastated by evidence of sexual abuse. I was confronted and mugged by two men on my way home. Six of our guests were pick-pocketed while visiting our new house. In addition, the church parking lot became the setting of a gun battle that ended with one man dead and another man injured. The shooting happened in the middle of the day while the parish school's principal and students were picking up litter on the grounds. It is fortunate that no one at the school was hurt.

    I try to avoid negative sensationalism, but sin is ugly. In the face of ugliness, we stand with the balm, the transformer, the re-birther: Love. The clash between love and sin is the drama of humanity. This drama is obvious and yet constantly forgotten. No word is too bad to describe sin. No word is worthy to describe love. One defies cursing, the other is beyond praise.

    As we live conscious of this drama, we should be careful not to oversimplify or reduce it unfairly. Sin and love are as polar as life and death, but they coexist in almost every human action. Even our sinful acts are messy corruptions of good by evil where the angels have fought for the inches. But God did not sacrifice Himself for partial victory. God sacrificed Himself to make us completely pure and holy.

To be pure and holy is to live in a straight forward manner and to open ourselves to God like a child. The Lord only asks us "to do justice, to love kindness, and to walk humbly" with Him (Mi 6:8). God has never requested anything that is not for our own good and that He is not willing to provide.

Evil in the world is the challenge that faces Christianity. We respond to this challenge with the good news of Christ and try to make our witness credible through our actions. Thank you for supporting the Christmas outreach. Christmas bags were delivered to 150 families, and in a separate outreach, Christmas gifts were angeled to over 75 children.

In January, we expanded to a second location in the Shaw neighborhood of Washington, DC. Our new house is drafty, and water leaks in whenever it rains. We are currently working on solving the water problem by replacing the gutters and having the back wall pointed and sealed.

In February, Laura Cartagena answered God's call to become the first live-in volunteer at the House of the Three Teresas. Laura has been involved with A Simple House since it was just an idea, and she served as the first chairman of our board. She is also leading our effort to transform the house into a suitable living space for more missionaries.

In March, we hosted a fish fry with Fr. Charles Pope speaking on "The Role of Scripture in Our Lives." Forty people crowded into a small room to enjoy the fellowship and inspiring talk. In addition, we welcomed alternative spring break groups from Mary Washington College and the University of Rochester, who helped paint rooms at the House of the Three Teresas.

All of this is in addition to our constant work of friendship ministry with the poor, which includes taking people to church, meeting with them in their homes, delivering food, meeting unique needs, and supporting new mothers. All of these works are ineffectual without love. When anything in our life becomes more important than love, it has become more important than God. Putting love first seems simple, and it is simple. The difficult thing is to not let it become complicated (Ecclus. 7:29). Simplicity requires courage.

Cooperating with God's work means becoming a saint, and it results in a paradoxical element in our lives. St. Francis of Assisi was often considered super serious, super dedicated, and super simple. Anything in his life that opposed the Lord came under the axe. This severity of St. Francis allowed him to be super light, irresponsible in the eyes of the world, and fancy free. His purity and holiness were childlike, but his necessary resolution was manly.

Thank you for making this ministry possible and reading our letters.

Clark Massey

> We must keep His interests continually in our hearts and minds, carrying our Lord to places where He has not walked before, fearless in doing the things He did, courageously going through danger and death with Him and for Him; ready to accept joyously the need to die daily if we want to bring souls to God, to pay the price He paid for souls – ever ready to go to any part of the world and to respect and appreciate unfamiliar customs of other peoples, their living conditions and language, willing to adapt ourselves if and when necessary, happy to undertake any labor and toil, and glad to make any sacrifice involved in our missionary life.

This imposes a great responsibility on us to fight against our own ego and love of comfort that would lead us to choose a comfortable and insignificant mediocrity. We are called upon to make our lives a rivalry with Christ; we are called upon to be warriors in saris, for the church needs fighters today. Our war cry has to be "Fight not flight."

>-Bl. Teresa of Calcutta

THE TWO WAYS

Dear Friends and Family,   June 2006

"Two Ways there are, one of Life and one of Death, and there is a great difference between the Two Ways." This is the first sentence of the oldest Christian document outside of the Bible, the Didache. This language is parallel to Christ's identity as "the Way, the Truth, and the Life" (Jn 14:6). We often think of "going to hell" as something that happens at the final judgment or as a rude accusation, but whenever we sin we are literally on the way to Hell. When we love, we are on the way to heaven. There is a great difference between the two ways, and we deceive ourselves when we think we have made a truce with sin. St. Augustine says, "On the road to God not to go forward is to go backward."

There is no such thing as the sin we need, the sin that helps a relationship, the sin that makes us happy. Every sin is unnecessary, destroys relationships, and makes us miserable. "The wages of sin is death" (Rom 6:23), and every honest reflection bears this out. Sin makes life not worth living.

Most people we minister to have been and are going through periods of alcoholism, drug abuse, or prostitution. The cause and result of these problems are often the same: sin. We need to help derail people who are on the way of death. Many of the men we serve have abandoned their children and wives to seek false comfort. Mothers and children we serve often feel betrayed and have a great need for love. Our ministry encourages fathers to make the right decision, and tries to support mothers materially and spiritually so that they have a greater ability to love and provide for their children. We love because we have first been loved. God gives us love, which is a reason to live. It is the reason to go to Heaven.

Because of the generosity of two new volunteers, Audrey O'Herron (who has moved into the House of the Three Teresas) and Aaron Maddeford, we are doing more ministry and more housework than ever before. [4]

Every week is different, but we try to create structure while responding to the particular needs that frequently arise. (I like to think of this flexibility as obedience to God's will.) In an ideal week, Tuesday, Thursday, and Saturday are used for ministry. Most of Sunday is filled with taking people to church. Two days each week are used to rehabilitate the House of the Three Teresas, and we defend one day each week as a day of rest.

The work on the House of the Three Teresas is extensive. Using volunteer labor and a few contractors, rooms have been patched and painted, the back wall of the house has been pointed, and new gutters have been installed to stop water from flowing into the house. Besides the ongoing work of plastering and painting, the house needs a new fence to stop drug use in the back yard and a complete fire alarm system with a control panel to meet DC rooming house requirements.

In late April, the Beachner family of Parsons, Kansas, donated a luxury passenger van. This gift was especially timely because in May our minivan was stolen, wrecked, and totaled by a group of men who then stole the police car that was chasing them. We are hoping to replace the minivan soon because it is difficult to work from two locations with only one vehicle.

---
[4] Clark Massey and Audrey O'Herron married on August 27, 2011.

The Gospels portray the apostles as a befuddled and fumbling group of men following Jesus. All of their worst mistakes and most embarrassing remarks seem to be recorded in the Gospels. There is a special evangelical teaching hidden in these stories. We know the apostles messed up because they told everyone how they messed up. The apostles used their personal weaknesses and defeats to testify about God's greatness. It takes humility and courage to talk about our mistakes and weaknesses, but it is our confessions which cut to the heart of our fellow man. It is less powerful (and less true) to say, "Follow God because it has sure worked out great for me!" than to say, "Despite all of my failed efforts, hardheartedness, and self-deceit, God keeps blessing me."

Thank you for being a blessing to me and this ministry.

Clark Massey

CHARITY IN TRUTH

Dear Friends and Family,   October 2006

    In our large cities and suburbs, it is very difficult for the rich and poor to build friendships. This situation keeps us from helping each other. As a result of not knowing the poor, the modern world often approaches the poor with uncharitable truth or untruthful charity.

    A Simple House is trying to serve the poor with charity and truth. To avoid ignorance, it is important to discuss the real struggles of the poor. It is also important to protect privacy and avoid gossip. Whenever a situation is described in our letters, the names are changed and no information is given to link a particular story with a particular family.

    We recently met the Campbells, an elderly couple who have been married for thirty years. Ten years ago, their house had an electrical fire, and the couple started repairing the damage on their own. Unfortunately, Mr. Campbell suffered a stroke, and it became necessary for him to use an oxygen pump. These infirmities left Mr. Campbell unable to climb the stairs and trapped him in the two upper rooms of the house. Mr. Campbell's illness stalled the renovation, and for the last decade, the Campbells have been living in the shell of a house where open walls expose pipes, wires, and insulation.

    The Campbells are private people, and it is only with a flexible and gentle ministry that people like the Campbells can receive the help they need. Mrs. Campbell confessed that they qualify for almost every program designed to help the elderly, but she is too busy at her job and caring for her husband to pursue help. Mr. Campbell should never be left at home alone, but this is a luxury they cannot afford. We help the Campbells by giving Mrs. Campbell rides and assistance signing up for aid. We have also started a project to close up the walls in their home.

Although volunteers can fix the interior walls, there are two holes in the roof which require a professional contractor. The Campbells cannot pay for this repair, and we do not currently have the funds to help them with this problem. Please pray that we will receive the funds to help the Campbells with their roof. When need is as extreme as this, it feels like a great honor to be able to provide assistance.

The Holley family is only a mother and daughter. The daughter is thirty years old and suffers from cerebral palsy which has shrunken and curled her body. The mother is her full-time nurse, and they live in a small apartment with a hospital bed. Although the daughter cannot speak, they appear to comprehend each other's needs and moods.

In early September, we took Ms. Holley to meet her daughter as she was coming out of surgery. When we arrived, the surgeon told Ms. Holley that her daughter would probably pass during the night. At this important time, our volunteers were the only people to comfort and help the mother. To our surprise, the daughter had been baptized as a Catholic (even though her mother is not Catholic). We found a priest to administer the last sacrament.

Even though her life was almost entirely hidden, large numbers of people attended her funeral to testify to her love and witness. It was impressive to see the powerful effect on others of a life lived in silence.

Because of your generosity, we were able to help support this family in their hour of need and defray some of the funeral costs.

There are many women prostituting themselves on the street in front of my house. They seem confused and rarely make sense when they talk. They do not like to make eye contact, and they often do not finish statements or answer friendly questions. Paradoxically, they seem to like being talked too. I have had the privilege to know a few of these women after they got off the street and were clean for a few months. They were new women. They talked intelligently and were very articulate. After admitting to one woman that I didn't really know that she could talk, she confessed that she was too ashamed to talk with people. Now that she was recovering and attending a church-based program, she was no longer ashamed.

Another woman whom I recognized from the street told me, "I have a real job!" This announcement was strange because out of politeness we had never openly talked about her fake job. Her attempt at being a cashier was short lived, but a few months later she disappeared from my street. After a long absence, I saw her walking down my street without "walking the street." I stopped her to talk, and it was the first time she was articulate, smart, and for the most part unashamed. She had been in a recovery program and started living in Virginia. She was revisiting my street to see if the old excitement and drama was still there. She admitted that it was no longer exciting and interesting; rather it greatly scared her. Realizing that she was on the brink of falling off the wagon, I offered her a ride home, but she would not take it. She was still looking for something on the street. A month later, it was clear that she had fallen back into prostitution. She now has a foot in both worlds. Please pray for her.

What We Are Doing

We are currently doing more work than we have ever done. Every month Simple House volunteers are packing and delivering over 75 bags of groceries, and in August, we delivered school supplies assembled by the freshman class of Visitation High School.

Short notice picnics for the families we serve have become a Simple House staple. We travel fifteen miles outside of DC to Great Falls National Park, and the family gets a tour of the falls, an outfitted catfishing expedition, a barbeque feast, and plenty of chucking the football. All of this begins and ends with prayer. One mother together with her six children caught 25", 23", 22", and 16" catfish and one medium-sized snapping turtle with Vienna sausage as bait. It is hard to place a value on the experience of bringing inner-city kids to a national park, giving a struggling family good family time, and letting the love of God shine through the project.

We are still focusing on the harder and more important work of helping people with religious reflection, studying the Bible, going to church, and hoping for the future. The spiritual works of mercy are the harder part of the ministry and the least quantifiable part of what we do.

Some Blessings Since June

The Missionaries of Charity (Mother Teresa's sisters) have been a long standing witness to us and our neighborhood. Their monastery is contemplative, but the sisters do outreach by walking through the neighborhood, knocking on doors, and praying with people. When they find a case of extreme need, they sometimes introduce Simple House volunteers to the family. In addition, the sisters have been very generous donors of food and supplies to A Simple House.

St. Mark Catholic Community of Vienna, VA, donated a missionary fellowship to provide the majority of financial support for our new full-time missionary, Jessica Hensle. Jessica graduated from Mary Washington College and found out about A Simple House from students who helped paint the House of the Three Teresas as an alternative spring break. Audrey O'Herron has moved out of the House of the Three Teresas but is continuing to volunteer part time as she starts her graduate studies at the Institute of Psychological Sciences (which specializes in studying psychology from a religious perspective). Since the last letter, Teresa Reardon, Natalie Regan, and Danny Shields have come on board as part-time volunteers.

The Newman Center at George Washington University sponsored a lasagna day for A Simple House. They made nine lasagnas and ten apple pies which were delivered to mothers raising families in the poorest neighborhoods of Washington, DC.

The Copley Crypt Church community of Georgetown donated a used minivan in order to replace the one that was stolen and then wrecked. Copley Crypt has also donated a missionary fellowship in honor of their former pastor, Fr. Paul Cioffi, SJ. This fellowship will support the work of Laura Cartagena as she serves as a full-time missionary.

In August, I was allowed to speak to a crowd of young adults at an Irish pub. The topic of my talk was "Letting Jesus Ruin Your Life." It was a humbling honor to be allowed to share Christ in this way, and I'm thankful it went well.

Clark Massey

GENEROSITY OF THE POOR

Dear Friends and Family,   December 2006

One of the most rewarding parts of our ministry is to witness the generosity of the poor. In neighborhoods full of broken homes, drug addiction, and crime, many children and teenagers live a life without supervision or a concerned parent. They are not sheltered or regularly fed. The confused depravity of the neighborhood is their school. No one knows the plight of these children better than the neighborhood mothers, and we have met many mothers who feed and take in children whenever a crisis arises. They act without hesitation, not counting the cost. They willingly give their own dinner to a hungry child and make an act of faith that God will provide for them and their family. God has given us the honor of being an emergency lifeline for these mothers. Your charity supports their charity.

A friend of the ministry experienced a very hard fought conversion, but after about a year, she succumbed to her old temptations. She met a man who promised many things and told many lies. He knowingly infected her with HIV, made her pregnant, robbed her, and fortunately left her. These new realities will stay with her even after she returns to the Church. Sin multiplied her crosses. Only Jesus can make the crosses light.

Our love for one another, like God's love for us, must be larger than sin. We cannot let temporary and almost inevitable setbacks break our heart or our friendship. We need to encourage people and bring them back into the body of the Church. It is fundamental to ministry to continue being someone's friend even if they fail and to let them know you will still be their friend if they fail. In this way, we image the Father's love.

During our Thanksgiving outreach, we met a family with no food. They had to use the Thanksgiving bag and gift card we delivered for the following day. We immediately invited them to our food pantry and gave them about two weeks' worth of canned goods. Thanks to the generosity of Erin Dublin, who won the Georgetown Turkey Trot, we were able to give them a prize turkey. They are a small family with a mother who is nearly paralyzed by depression. This paralysis keeps her from taking advantage of the many organizations set up to help the poor.

We met another family in a similar situation. Their home is always dark, and the children are neglected due to the mother's depression. After an altercation, the oldest daughter murdered the mother's boyfriend. She was released after a year in jail to raise her own child and help her mother. People in situations of great need rarely wander into a church or look for real help. They must be searched for. The people who know of families in such desperate straits are their neighbors, and the way to find them is by networking in a neighborhood or through door-to-door outreaches. When they are discovered, we need to bring Jesus to them through our words and actions.

Thank you for making these outreaches possible, and thank you for making the follow-up and everyday ministry of A Simple House possible.

We have just completed our "Everything but the Bird" Thanksgiving outreach to over 150 families in three separate neighborhoods. It was made possible by volunteers, your donations, and the generosity of Visitation High School. A special thanks goes to Jessica Hensle for coordinating the outreach. A special thanks also goes to Officer John Reardon and his daughter Teresa who used a patty wagon to deliver turkeys to some of the families we serve.

It was unfortunate and distressing that we ran short of Thanksgiving bags and were unable to fully cover our target neighborhoods and the other families we serve. In order to correct this problem, we are hoping to create and distribute 175 Christmas bags. We also hope to angel and deliver gifts to over one hundred children and mothers. We need your support to make this possible.

Since the last newsletter: Our empty food pantry was replenished by food drives at Visitation High School and Archbishop Carroll High School. Volunteers visited six universities to attract applicants for next year's missionary fellowship program. I gave a talk at the Newman Center of George Washington University and the University of Kansas Catholic men's club. We also received visits from members of the New Meadow Run Bruderhof (an intentional Christian community in Pennsylvania) and students from the University of Mary Washington.

Our guests from the Bruderhof provided a delicious dinner and good conversation for volunteers, and they donated books on forgiveness for our Thanksgiving bags. The students from the University of Mary Washington visited A Simple House as part of their Urban Plunge. During the visit, they received a tour of the roughest neighborhoods of Washington, DC and assembled Thanksgiving bags.

In late November, we welcomed Ryan Hehman as a new live-in volunteer. Ryan graduated from the

Catholic University of America last May and has done ministry with "The House" at CUA, Andre House in Phoenix, AZ, and Exodus Youth Services (one of the inspirations of A Simple House) in Washington, DC.

Thank you for all the blessings you shower upon us.

Clark Massey

LIFE

Dear Friends and Family,   December 2006

    My name is Jessica Hensle, and I've been a full-time volunteer with A Simple House since August. Clark asked me to write about my experience with one of the girls we know. She's seventeen years old, and the mother of a beautiful one-year-old girl. About three months ago, Clark found out she was pregnant and had decided to get an abortion. He tried to talk with her, but she was not open to discussion. Although Laura and I didn't know her, Clark asked us to visit. Because we were terrified and felt inadequate, we asked some friends and nuns to pray for us and for the mother. The next morning we took her to IHOP. To our surprise she was open with us and receptive to the idea of keeping her child. A radical change from the day before! We committed to giving her rides to prenatal appointments and helping with diapers and food. It was a wonderful feeling to know God's grace had prevailed.

    Over the next couple of months we took her to several appointments. This gave us a lot of time to talk and pray, establishing what has become a close friendship and a personal blessing. She is a very bright girl, with a good sense of humor and a good heart.

    During her third trimester, Laura and I took her to a regularly scheduled appointment. After sitting in the waiting room for a while, we were called back and told there was "bad news." When we opened the door she was sobbing. The doctors were unable to find the baby's heartbeat and would have to induce labor. Although some friends and family visited throughout the evening, by 10 o'clock everyone else had gone home. Seeing the lack of support she received, I was glad I could be there as a friend.

    Shortly after midnight she gave birth to a stillborn little boy. Once she and the baby were cleaned up, the nurse brought him over for her to hold. She asked if I'd like to hold him. When I did, I was surprised to feel how light he was, only 1 pound, 6 ounces.

    For the next couple of hours she tried to call her mother without success. At around three in the morning, the nurse brought the baby over for the mother to hold one last time. Then the nurse placed him in a little bag and took him away.

    The family had no money for a funeral. Fortunately, a Catholic funeral home donated their services, so the baby's body was treated with the dignity it deserved. The family is not a member of any church and had no way to memorialize the child, so we offered to host a memorial dinner at A Simple House. Clark and some of the family members spoke, we sang a hymn, and shared a meal. It was a beautiful opportunity for the young mother and her family to honor the child as a human being and member of their family.

In Christ,

Jessica Hensle

OLD TESTAMENT WORLD

Dear Friends and Family,   Easter 2007

    In the last six months, DeAndre has been shot in the head twice, but he is doing fine. DeAndre is two hundred pounds overweight, and he doesn't move very fast. Both incidents took place while he was sitting on his front porch, and neither of the bullets penetrated his skull. The first incident involved a stray bullet from a drive-by shooting. A few months later, another stray bullet went through his front door, and in December, he was shot in the head again. This time DeAndre was the target, but the motive was unclear.

    It's improbable that someone would be shot in the head twice in six months, and it's even more improbable that the person would come away without any serious injury. When DeAndre attended a court date about the second shooting, friends of the shooter verbally taunted him, and one threatened him by making a gun with his hand. This happened in front of police officers and a US marshal. DeAndre decided not to testify, and the DC government transferred him to a different project neighborhood. Please pray that his family remains safe and that these events will lead them closer to Christ.

    Five young men from our neighborhood have been in multiple GED programs without success. Over the last couple of months, we have hosted eight study days. Each day starts with over an hour of Bible study followed by lunch and academic tutoring. Our math and language arts studies often suffer when we have breakthrough conversations during the Bible study.

Studying the Bible with these young men is very enjoyable. The ideas in the Bible are fresh to them, and they confront the ideas without passing over time-worn words or phrases. All of them are on their way to intellectually affirming the truth, but they are still waiting to put it into practice.

The day after a recent study session, one of the men was attacked and robbed while standing at the bus stop with his three-year-old nephew. After a brief fight, he lay unconscious with his nephew standing over him. His ear had to be stitched back together, and his jaw and face were bruised and scraped up.

Unlike the incredible incidents that happened to DeAndre, there is probably a simple explanation for our friend being attacked. His assailants claimed that they were seeking revenge, and although he didn't remember them, he admits that he may have done the same thing to one of them.

DeAndre and the men in our study group have grown up in neighborhoods that are similar to the Old Testament world of Abraham. Abraham lived in fear that he would be murdered and his wife raped. In fact, she was taken from him and released several times, and on another occasion, he had to bring his family to war in order to save his nephew's family from abduction and slavery. Abraham's world did not have dependable structures for enforcing justice, and crime often appeared lucrative and glorious. Throughout all of this, Abraham lived a heroic life of virtue and was a friend of God. Most of our society has been formed by Christian thought, and although we risk mild persecutions, the Christian virtues are usually rewarded not only by God but by our society. This is less true in an inner-city neighborhood. These men need to be formed into Christian heroes and friends of God who do right despite the consequences.

Christmas was a great blessing for our ministry. Your generosity allowed us to give gifts to over 100 children and distribute Christmas baskets to 175 families. Visitation High School blessed us by donating all of the food items in our Christmas baskets. In addition, we were blessed with some generous financial gifts which allowed us to do repairs at the House of the Three Teresas (the ceiling was caving in, and the floor is infested with termites), give some beds and furniture to needy families, and acquire two used minivans. One of the vans is being used for ministry, and the other van was given to a family of nine as their first vehicle.

In addition to our regular ministry and study sessions, we have started hosting game nights for neighborhood friends. Game nights have become the winter equivalent of our summer fishing trips and are excellent opportunities to combine ministry and fun.

Thank you for praying for this ministry and for the blessings you shower upon us.

Clark Massey

CONVERSION

Dear Friends and Family,   July 2007

Our ministry has been close friends with a family for over three years. In May, six members of the family were baptized and received into the Church. This is an amazing blessing. Laura Cartagena and I are the new godparents. This is the first (and sixth) time I've become a godfather. It's awesome.

Also in May, a boy was murdered. We had met and prayed with the boy multiple times, but we did not know him or his family well. In a separate drive-by shooting, another boy closer to our ministry was shot in the head. The bullet is still in his head, but he has mostly recovered. These boys were high school friends, and their other friends, who range in age from 13 to 19, are leading a lifestyle centered on guns, drugs, and a strange sense of valor. If they do not leave this street lifestyle, there will be more deaths over the next few years. Please pray for these boys. Pray that "street life" will be revealed as miserable and replaced with life in Christ.

Life in Christ needs to be the highest priority for all of us, but we are often afraid to completely give ourselves to the Lord. We avoid God and fear death because we want to preserve a distorted part of ourselves which will not withstand the presence of God. "No one can see the face of God and live" (Ex 33:20). This part of us is a false self-image. It is a little idol we create that is not worthy of the true self which God created.

In the desert, Moses destroyed the Israelites' idol, a golden calf. He burned it, crushed it, pounded it to powder, mixed it with water, and made everyone drink it down (Ex 32:20). This have-no-mercy approach is the only way to approach our own little idols.

When our idols are gone and we have fully come to terms with God, there is no reason to fear death. Death is for our good. Death is the opportunity to start over and leave this imperfect, always lacking, and often painful world. The gift of Jesus is peace, and this peace opens the door of heaven, puts us in touch with our true selves, and makes it unnecessary to avoid God and fear death.

As a ministry, we continually have to start all over following Christ. We are tempted to get off mission by only meeting the immediate material needs of families. Recently our food pantry experienced explosive growth with more people than ever calling to request food and visits.

Meeting only material needs is easier, more quantifiable, and in the short run more gratifying for the missionary. In this way, we are tempted to abandon the mission and delude ourselves that we are the savior of the poor. This attitude is unchristian and a recipe for burnout.

Our mission focuses on spiritual poverty rather than material poverty. There are many food pantries and agencies in DC which make food available to people in need. When we find a hungry family, it is usually caused by a neglectful parent who may suffer from mental illness or drug abuse. Our mission is to use friendship evangelization powered by God's grace to address spiritual poverty while still meeting the immediate material needs of the family. Your financial generosity and prayers make this possible.

Through your generosity, we now have two canoes, and our ministry fishing trips have expanded to new horizons. We now take families to national parks and paddle to beaches which are not accessible by roads. We also broadened our expeditions to include clamming and crabbing. Some of the neighborhood kids have started a "lemonade stand" type business selling clams. On our outings, they get to swim, have fun, and work as entrepreneurs all at the same time.

Since the last letter, the House of the Three Teresas was broken into, and our tools and fishing poles were stolen. In the same neighborhood, one of our volunteers was attacked late at night. The House of the Three Teresas is in a wealthier and therefore "safer" part of town, but the area appears to be targeted for muggings and break-ins. Since then, we have invested in a security door, and we no longer let volunteers or visitors walk to their cars alone after dark. Please pray for the safety of our ministry.

Thank you for supporting us. May Christ's peace be with you.

Clark Massey

FAMILY SUPPORT

Dear Friends and Family,   October 2007

    The first few chilly days of fall have arrived. This summer flew by faster than any summer I can remember. It was full of many blessings and wonderful opportunities for me. I got to see a lot of friends and family. In the middle of what has been maybe the most spiritually and emotionally trying time of my life, I was able to visit the families of my friends at their homes in the mountains, at the beach, and on farms. I was invited to many delicious dinners and relaxing places. God has not forsaken me, and looking back on the summer I see all the "pick-me-ups" that he showered on me through the hospitality and generosity of so many people.

    The summer brought blessings in our ministry as well. Two mothers we know gave birth to healthy babies. We were given the privilege of picking them up from the hospital and taking the babies home for the first time.

    Another wonderful thing is that we worked with several families to enroll their children in Catholic schools in the city. With the help of different scholarships and school vouchers, these kids have had a huge door opened to them. By going to Catholic schools these children will be removed from the poor education, violence, sexual harassment, and low graduation rates which are found in most DC public schools. We were also able to help many other kids by providing them with school supplies. Georgetown

Visitation High School helped us pack and decorate 150 bags of supplies which we distributed the first week of school.

One of my favorite things from the summer was my visit to the Bruderhof community in Western Pennsylvania with two of the girls who were baptized last spring with me and Clark as the godparents. We were welcomed with homemade cookies and cards. We spent the weekend with the Domer family who took us fishing, on pony cart rides, to a campfire, and to other community events. It was a chance for two girls who have barely been out of the city to see mountains, farms, and animals that are not rats. It was also a chance for us to witness Christianity lived out radically.

Reflecting on my summer made me realize how fortunate I am. I am fortunate to have the opportunities to do and see many things. I am fortunate that so many people welcome me to be a part of their lives. I am fortunate to have so many friends and family who support me when I need it. If I have good news or bad news, if I am ever in a bind or have a problem, someone is always there to help me. I have always had this, have always expected it, and have always taken it for granted.

This highlights a sharp contrast between the support that I've grown up with and the support many of the poor experience. It was striking this summer to know that there are so many places I can go and people to take care of me. I was at the same time struck by how my goddaughters had never traveled anywhere that they saw mountains on the horizon until they visited the Bruderhof. In fact, even many of the adults we work with haven't seen mountains on the horizon. Trips away from the city are so cherished and rare that we often hear people speak of trips long ago as if they just took place. And though I felt honored to be taking a baby home for the first time, it was strange that I was part of such an intimate moment. Had I been in the hospital, I would have had a line of friends and family willing and able to take me home.

    Many of us have grown up with a network of support and safety nets which many of the families we serve do not have. There are many circumstances that make the poor in Southeast unreliable. Those we serve and their families often live from check to check each month. Managing food stamps, bills, and kids going to school can each become a little or a very large emergency every month. Add to this struggles with drug use, absent family members, and lack of transportation. When you or the people around you are regularly dealing with these kinds of problems, it is difficult if not impossible to find dependability. I've always taken for granted that if I were ever in a bind there would always be a backup plan, ultimately leading to my parents who would do what they could to bail me out. I cannot imagine a time when my parents would not be there to do so, and if there was, even then, there would be another back up plan. My parents have always made sure that I am okay. They have provided me with the best education possible. They've enabled me to see and do many things beyond our home. Along with so many people, they have been there when I am sad, or worried, or confused.

    When I think of the difficult times in my life, it is hard for me to imagine what they would be like without all my friends and family who have been so consistent and generous. I can only imagine how easy it would be for my hope and joy to be replaced by great fear and despair. We need to bring hope where there is fear and love where there is loneliness. While material goods can be a great help, they do not provide as much for a person as knowing that there is someone there for them and that they're not alone. I think that this is how we need to bring Christ to the poor. We are all poor in the sense that we are all in need of love. So many times in my life I've experienced love as somebody to count on or be there. We need to be that for each other, and in a special way, for those who have no one else to fill this role.

With love in Christ,

Laura Cartagena

VOLUNTARY POVERTY

Dear Friends and Family,　　　　　　　　October 2007

It's been a long, hot summer here in DC, or as my mom affectionately calls it, "the swamp." While this may not be a foreign mission in the jungles of the Amazon, life at T Street does present some unique challenges. Just the thought of living in this city without air-conditioning is enough to make most people break into a sweat. Thankfully, the constant whir of our fans distracts us from the near-constant buzz of mosquitoes.

Since the summer began, we have waged ongoing battles to rid our house of all sorts of pesky intruders and fortify our defenses. I am pleased to report that Jess and I recently walked away the victors of a head-to-head giant rat vs. human showdown in the kitchen. Unfortunately, while we rested on our laurels, the ants marched in and annexed my carpet and some of my drawers. On top of it all, the past few weeks have been lean ones for our ministry, giving us the opportunity to invent many new dishes in our garbanzo-bean cuisine.

Although stories like these provide hours of amusement for my friends, sometimes I just want to add, "but seriously, this stinks." At times I get the feeling that I didn't really know about everything I was signing up for when I came to A Simple House.

In fact, the question of why I live here and observe voluntary poverty – with all its challenges and surprises – is one that I ask myself often. Are we simply trying to emulate the lifestyle of the poor, or is there more to the idea of living in solidarity with the poor than mere imitation? What good is "going without?"

Solid answers to these questions often elude me. But the answer to why I do these things is simply less important than the fact that I have been invited by Christ to do them. Our aim in abandoning unnecessary luxuries and simplifying our lives is to be more aware of our blessings, to love God with undivided hearts, to cling to Christ and learn from Him. Still, this is often an uphill battle. And this summer I found, like the poor, that it is difficult to listen to the voice of God when the noise and disruptions of daily life threaten to drown Him out.

Despite this similarity, the poor we serve live in poverty for a different reason and in different ways. Last Christmas, we were introduced to a new family through the Missionaries of Charity. Ruth, a single white mother who has adopted and raised two black children with special needs, lives in a sizeable three-bedroom house in Anacostia. Though they have plenty of living space, it is cluttered with trash and infested with roaches. Depression, disease, and the demands of raising her boys have taken their toll on Ruth and have manifested themselves in these living conditions. So when we pitched the idea of cleaning up the house and renting a steam cleaner for the carpet, she beamed. On a Saturday morning in August, a few part-time volunteers and I teamed up with Ruth's sons to tackle the project.

The Holy Spirit blessed us with a beautiful experience. The volunteers, none of whom had yet done much ministry with A Simple House, responded lovingly and wholeheartedly to Ruth and her sons, despite the dirty tasks we had to do. Cleaning the house turned out to be a great way to hang out with the family for the day. We got to know more about the boys and their interests and spent valuable time with Ruth as well, who is often busy taking care of the younger neighborhood boys (most of whom call her Mom).

This type of Christian love—a unique help meeting a unique need—is important to our concept of what it means to serve the poor. Being able to sit down with a family, ask what they need, and think of original ways to meet that need is a privilege that few social service organizations have. There is no one-size-fits-all solution to the problems of the poor. Love, in its many different expressions, requires authentic relationship if it is to bear the fruit of growth and change in our lives and the lives of those we serve.

Ideally, the relationship we build with God through prayer and the sacrifice of voluntary poverty inspires us to serve and know the poor in new and creative ways. Over the summer, we experimented with a small expansion of the ministry to the homeless living around our T Street neighborhood and farther downtown. As the weather cools, we hope to spend a little more time meeting with homeless friends on the street and providing a sandwich, a coke, some laughter, and some prayer.

In other news, we are glad to welcome Kelly Pertee, our new full-time volunteer from Columbus, Ohio. Kelly graduated from Ohio Dominican University in 2006 and has volunteered for St. Paul's Outreach in Columbus as a college youth minister.

In order to spread the word to others like Kelly, I recently took a trip to the Midwest to attend volunteer fairs at Loyola University of Chicago, Marquette University, and Notre Dame. In addition to meeting enthusiastic students, it was a great way to network with other organizations and spread the word about some of the work we are undertaking here in DC.

Thank you for all of your support, and know that you are in our prayers.

In Christ,

Ryan Hehman

PROSPERITY

Dear Friends and Family,   Christmas 2007

    The Williams family has thirteen children and lives in a four bedroom apartment. On a recent visit, Ryan and I delivered school supplies and food. At the end of the visit, Mrs. Williams requested prayer for her children's success in school and for prosperity. Eight of the children were holding hands in a prayer circle, and a few of them said, "Prosperity?" Ryan and I were getting ready to explain the meaning of the word prosperity until another child shouted for Prosperity, and a four-year-old girl ran out of the back room to join the prayer.

    We have known the Williams family for a few years. They happily receive everything that is offered but never ask for help despite their obvious need. Their need has to speak for itself. A few months ago, the father left the family, and what was a difficult task for two people has been left to the mother.

    The Williams' greatest need is a larger place to live in a safer neighborhood. (The front door of their apartment building has been shot out multiple times.) Our goal is to help this family move by the end of January. This type of special project relies on the extraordinary generosity of our donors and volunteers. Thank you.

    "Treat everyone with equal kindness; never be condescending but make real friends with the poor. Do not allow yourself to become self-satisfied" (Rom 12:16). Many people see the poor with apprehension and reservation, but to love God is to love the work of His hands. A Christian cannot say, "God you are all good and perfect, but you created a bunch of repugnant people." A lover of God loves his fellow men, and this is a prerequisite for salvation (Mt 25:31–46).

Befriending the poor is a way God purifies our love. Recognizing ourselves as their equal humbles us and keeps us from becoming self-satisfied and condescending. It is an honor to befriend the poor as God befriends them. This is the goal of our work.

Two young women we know have been working on college applications. Both of these students have been through many more trials than the average teenager. One of them experienced three evictions and long periods of homelessness during her high school career. Your generosity has helped her family many times over the past three years. Her graduation is an amazing success story and a bright spot in her family's struggles.

To make sure that these young women stay on track, Simple House volunteers are encouraging them and helping them complete the necessary forms. We are also still searching for the perfect graduation presents.

Volunteers at A Simple House try to have a weekly intellectual development meeting. Sometimes this meeting is our book club and other times it involves discussing an article or trying to grasp the true foundations of charitable work. Pope Benedict has frequently instructed Christians on how to serve the poor, and his writings have been very encouraging to our volunteers.

In Pope Benedict's latest book, *Jesus of Nazareth*, he talks about keeping Christ at the forefront of all work. He writes, "When God is regarded as a secondary matter that can be set aside temporarily or permanently on account of more important things, it is precisely these supposedly more important things that come to nothing." He also notes that:

> at the heart of all temptations . . . is the act of pushing God aside because we perceive Him as secondary, if not actually superfluous and annoying, in comparison with all the apparently far more urgent matters that fill our lives. Constructing a world by our own lights, without reference to God, building on our own foundation; refusing to acknowledge the reality of anything beyond the political and material, while setting God aside as an illusion—that is the temptation that threatens us in many varied forms.

Over the last hundred years, there has been a movement to secularize charitable work. When secular charities and welfare programs ignore the premises of Christianity and replace the Christian idea of person with a materialistic idea, they ignore an essential dimension of man's being and his reason for existence.

Truly effective charity must be God-centered and grace-fed. Please pray for us and pray that all welfare and charitable organizations will foster true love and not be afraid to draw on their Christian roots.

May Christ's peace be with you.

Clark Massey

JARRELL'S DEATH

Dear Friends and Family, October 2008

At the end of August, a new volunteer and I dropped in on the Atkins family, the first family I met in Southeast, DC. Upon our arrival we were greeted warmly by Mr. and Mrs. Atkins and Jarrell, their cousin who lived next door. I had just recently gotten to know Jarrell and this morning he seemed particularly happy and talkative.

The purpose of our visit was to organize rides for the annual Atkins family barbecue to be held the next day. A brother in the family who has "made it" would host the barbecue at his house in the Maryland suburbs, and he asked us to shuttle some of the family members who otherwise had no way to get there. We were happy to oblige, hopeful for the added bonus of getting some authentic soul food out of the deal. Although the conversation during our visit centered mostly around logistics, friendly banter, and "catching up," it was punctuated with serious discussion about the most recent neighborhood violence and one of the couple's sons who has been incarcerated for some time. Before we left, we prayed together as usual, and I noticed that Jarrell solemnly voiced a few serious intentions. After a warm goodbye, we drove away, riding high on the graces of a good visit.

The next morning, I was told that Jarrell had been shot and killed around the block from his home, just two days before his 28th birthday. When I received the news, I was shocked and saddened. Although A Simple House has dealt with death in the past, street violence has never claimed someone I knew so well. I sat for a moment, speechless, trying to put words to the feelings you feel when death steals someone quickly and unexpectedly from your presence. I was surprised by my own emotions because, until then, I thought I had seen and heard it all. No matter how accustomed–or how hardened–we may become to the effects of drugs and crime, the tragedy of a violent and untimely death always breaks through. It disrupts the peace we have struck with our world and challenges the meaning we give to our lives.

As reality sank in, I said a prayer for Jarrell and began to feel relief and consolation that he opened his heart to prayer during his last day here on earth. Moreover, I was awestruck and honored that we were given that moment to share with him.

That week, we participated in two major family events with the Atkins clan: the family barbecue and Jarrell's funeral. The barbecue went on as planned, and two months later there is still talk about the barbecued pork, inflatable moon-bounce, and the soul-train dance line. (In case you're wondering, I stunned the crowd with a moonwalk/robot dance-move combo the likes of which this city has never seen. In fact, I'm sure they'll never want to see it again, either.) A few days later, we celebrated Jarrell's life with the family during his funeral and helped prepare a repast at their house afterwards. Despite the difficulty, this week was a time of great family love and unity. But the fact remains that Jarrell is a casualty of a violent street culture. For the young men in the family still caught up in the street life, I pray his death is a catalyst for change in their lives.

Throughout both of these events, we were warmly welcomed and thanked for our presence and help. I was touched to be welcomed so deeply and graciously into the Atkins family because culture, upbringing, and skin color routinely remind me that I would not belong to such a family if not for Love. As missionaries, we depend on the invitation of others to enter into their homes and into their lives. We are undeservedly given the honor of being a guest in the lives of those we serve, but with Jarrell's death, I am beginning to see that this is a loaded invitation. How can I possibly prepare myself to meet the loneliness, despair, rejection, loss or whatever else I might find on the other side of that door?

Then again, who knows my worries better than Jesus, the Great Guest? Just as we depend on the invitation of others, Christ depends on our invitation. He stands at each of our doors, waiting to be invited in and to be counted as part of our family. Once invited, He listens as we talk, experiencing our joys and our pains as His own. Although He sees how messy our homes are, He does not force change. He does not bust in, broom and dustpan in hand, insistent that we get to work. He is simply interested in us. Once He's got our attention, however, He counts on our participation to make us new, to reset our priorities, and to change how we look at our lives and ourselves. When we finally realize Who is sitting in our living room, how can we neglect picking up a little for Him?

All relationships revolve around an invitation. Though there is uncertainty on both sides of the door, there is no love, growth, change, or joy in life if we never cross the threshold. Jarrell's death opened my eyes to the incredible importance of the invitations we receive. When families open their doors to us, who bring only groceries and watermelons, do they get any closer to opening their hearts to Christ, who brings salvation? The "success" of our ministry has little to do with how many watermelons we deliver or if each grocery bag is dropped off on time. The life of a Christian, like the life of Christ, has only one focus–relationship with the Other. Our success in life depends ultimately on the love in our encounters, which in turn depends on our encounter with the One True Friend.

In Christ,

Ryan Hehman

ROACHES

Dear Friends and Family,   October 2008

    As some of you may know, since the beginning of August I have been living in Southeast DC and working as a Christian missionary with a group called A Simple House. We are a community of Catholic volunteers trying to follow the Lord through voluntary poverty and love of the poor. Basically, we go around making and sustaining friendships with people in the name of Christ.

    This description may seem simple, but I keep marveling that I'm doing this at all. I can't even remember crossing the Anacostia River before, let alone driving into project neighborhoods to meet with people in their living rooms. It probably sounds crazy. In a way though, what A Simple House does isn't all that extraordinary. We're just trying to be Christians.

    In cultivating friendships, we find ourselves doing all sorts of things to respond to the unique needs of the families around us. For instance, I am the camping director and have organized multiple camping and fishing trips for our friends. We also deliver food, help clean houses, give rides to appointments, or just hang out. So while the differences in culture and background are sometimes daunting, it isn't hard to realize that we have more in common than not. We all experience loneliness, joy, and sorrow, and we were all made for love. I find myself thinking about these things in my relationships with a woman named Sharon and her two teenage sons, Adam and Mark.

Sharon suffers from depression, physical disabilities, and the stress of raising two kids with special needs; these factors paralyze her and keep her from living more fully. The state of her house makes this clear. With all of Sharon's other cares, the family's living situation has become serious. Recently, Sharon asked us for any kind of help we could give. In response, we offered to come clean and paint part of her house.

On a Friday morning, four of us arrived at Sharon's house ready to spend the day cleaning and painting. Little did we know of the great battle that would ensue, but the roaches had even less warning. Our forces undertook the first courageous assault, which involved targeting the piles of trash and junk where the enemy dared to congregate in plain sight. Perhaps this manner of describing the day appears too light, but the hardest part of the job was trying not to look grossed out. The best way I found to combat this was to smile and laugh, taking everything in stride. Besides, it did feel more like waging war on the house than anything else.

After the initial foray into the enemy's territory calmed down, we found ourselves separated amidst the struggle. Each one of us fought on in fearful places such as the living room, the closet, and, though I shudder to mention it, behind the refrigerator. At times, some of us would cleave a path toward one another on the battlefield, reuniting to launch a common attack. It was in this way that Ryan Hehman and I besieged and vanquished the roach stronghold on the underside of the dining room table. He masterfully wielded bleach and Raid while I blocked the futile attempts of escape with my faithful Shop-Vac. So it was that the battle raged until late in the afternoon. In the end, nearly the entire main floor found itself conquered and transformed.

Throughout the day, the focus was not only on the cleaning. One of us always managed to stay by Sharon, spending time with her rather that becoming caught up in the work itself. Not wanting to come in as a cleaning service but as friends offering a gift, the importance of keeping Sharon involved cannot be overemphasized. Once the day's work had finished, we gathered with the family to pray before returning home to reflect on what had taken place.

The question inevitably came up, "Why do we do this?" Given that A Simple House had cleaned the same house in the past, and it went back to its normal state after a few weeks, why bother with it again? Sharon came to us asking for help. This is what we offered. She made herself vulnerable to us, allowing us to enter into her suffering in a wonderfully intimate way, and afterwards, her thankfulness made it quite apparent. The next visit showed the fruits of the cleaning day. Sharon talked with us for over two hours about her life, God, the Bible, and her concerns about her boys. The hope is to visit the family once a week and do some maintenance cleaning with Adam and Mark, in order to help them form better habits.

Why do we concentrate so much on building relationships anyway? The problems that beset all of us do not have their final remedy in any material thing. Sharon and her boys do not primarily need food, clothing, and shelter–they thirst for friendship and love. Of course God wants His people to have the necessities of life, and A Simple House is glad to pass on whatever comes into our hands. But the human heart yearns for more. Human beings find their fulfillment and salvation in relationships with others. By aspiring toward love, they image God to one another and help open each other to the saving love of the redeemer, Jesus Christ. The moral life does not mean following arbitrary dictates in hopes of securing a distant reward. It draws us closer to living as our true selves, children of God united in love to one another and the Lord. Simple House strives to spark hope and the will to love in the hearts of others. Without this emphasis, all our labors would crumble, and we would merely be handing out band-aids.

May God give you peace,

Ryan Fredrickson

FIXING PROBLEMS

Dear Friends and Family,   Easter 2008

At the end of each home visit, we offer prayer. When we ask, "What would you like to pray for?" we often hear, "Pray that I can move," or "for help with my alcohol problem," or "that my baby's father will come around." Sometimes we hear, "Pray for our survival." We are rarely asked to pray for a permanent and peaceful home, complete healing from an addiction or illness, or a stable father who will dedicate himself in marriage. Sometimes we fail to even think of offering these prayers for our friends. We don't trust God's power and goodness even though Jesus promises, "I have come that you might have life and have it to the full" (Jn 10:10).

Why do we fail to trust Him? It is because we do not believe that we are desperately loved. We think that He wants to give us limited gifts even though He gives Himself entirely on the Cross and in the Eucharist. He even "eagerly desires" to do so (Lk 22:15).

At A Simple House we try to address these deeper issues through a ministry of friendship evangelization. We show our friends that they are greatly loved not only by us but, more importantly, by God. As Mother Teresa said, "What the poor need even more than food and clothing and shelter (though they need these, too, desperately) is to be wanted."

I recently took a friend to a pregnancy center to get her baby clothes and diapers. She's twenty-four years old and about to have her fifth child. Originally, she wasn't going to keep the baby. The other day, we were standing in her apartment talking about the difficulties of this pregnancy. As a "solution," I offered to take her back to the center for some more things. She had been packing to move and her couches were full of boxes overflowing onto the floor. She just pointed and said, "Jess, I think I have enough stuff." I can't explain how ridiculous I felt in that moment! I failed to realize that her anxiety was not primarily over material things. She is more deeply distressed that the previous fathers of her children have put her aside and that the new one is not returning her calls. She is experiencing a horrible feeling of being unloved, unwanted, and abandoned, along with a deep sense of shame. None of these issues can be fixed by anything. Ultimately, they must be healed by Someone.

Our friendship is an introduction to Him. As Pope Benedict says, "When we bring people only knowledge, ability, technical competence and tools [I would add groceries, diapers, clothes] we bring them too little." When we bring our friends love and the God who is Love, we bring the one necessary thing, "the good portion, which shall not be taken away" (Lk 10:42).

Please continue to pray for us and for our friends.

Jessica Hensle

FORGIVENESS

Dear Friends and Family,   Easter 2008

    I have been thinking about the love and mercy Jesus has for all of us. The Lord will forgive us for anything we have done if we accept His mercy. The simple request of the thief on the cross and Jesus' response that he would be in paradise illustrate Christ's mercy (Lk 23:40–43). The Lord gives the same mercy to us if we will accept it. His abundant mercy comes directly from His abundant love. We are called to pour out all of the love He gives us to others. As I pondered these things, I recalled recent events in my life where God has shown His love and mercy.

    Our friend Diana has had a hard life. She used to live in Alaska where she had a nice house, a family, and a job as a real estate agent. The details of her life are hard to piece together, but she lost everything and ended up homeless in DC. A few years ago, she was blessed with housing. She has a good heart and wants to help others as much as possible, but her past experiences have left her with bitterness, anger, and the question "Why did this have to happen to me?" This is all that she thinks about, and in a recent visit, she cried out, "I do not understand why I am like this, and why everyone rejects me!" The human heart can be very lonely when it feels like everything has been taken away. The only solution to this problem is Jesus Christ. Without Him, some situations do not make sense and tempt us to despair. In Him and through Him, we can hope. Fr. Raniero Cantalemessa, O.F.M Cap., explains that it is by the cross that Christ conquered Satan and all of his works. Now, by the cross, everything that Satan tries to do becomes a victory for Christ in His Divine Providence. We must believe that the power of Christ on the cross has the ability to conquer Satan and bring good out of everything he tries to do.

    Christ is showing His victory in Diana's life. She came to church with us one Sunday and grace began to flow through her. Afterwards, she decided to go on a pilgrimage and began to confront and forgive all that happened in her past. Praise be to God for His love and His mercy. He shows us every day that we can forgive others and turn back to Him.

    Helena is 70 years old and lives with us at the House of the Three Teresas. Helena spends her days sitting on our front steps or in the kitchen. She has a hard time walking, and she might have schizophrenia. Her ailments prevent her from doing things I take for granted. A couple of months ago, we felt the need to contact a social worker because we were not sure if Helena needed a different environment for her medical needs. Since then, she has received a guardian who will decide if Helena should stay with us or move. It has been very stressful for her as doctors, social workers, and lawyers come to see her. All of us want the best for her, but it is painful to think that she might not be here in the future. Ryan pointed out how lucky we are to have Helena with us. Every day we have the opportunity to serve Christ and to love Him by loving Helena. Although it is hard to come home from a day of serving the poor and continue to serve, it is what we are called to do as Christians. Christ gives us everything we need to live a Christian life, and everything we give to Him also comes from Him.

Thank you for your support of our little ministry and making everything we do possible.

Kelly Pertee

GOING OUT WEST

Dear Friends and Family,   Summer 2008

    God willing, A Simple House will open a new house in Kansas City, MO, this January. Kansas City was chosen because of the need amongst the poor and the support of our donors and volunteers in the area. In addition, Fr. Adam Ryan, OSB, who is a Simple House board member, is a monk at an abbey near Kansas City.

    A year ago, expansion was a long shot. We needed more volunteers, a house, and more money in order to expand. Without previous recruiting success (our largest recruiting class was only one person), six new volunteers will start in August, and although we hadn't even started looking, a generous donor offered us a house in Kansas City. Expansion has become a reality. The only missing factor is money. God has never made us do without, but it has been close at times.

    A Simple House had an extreme moment in its financial history last December. We did not have enough money to pay the bills, finish the preparations for Christmas, or give volunteers their stipends. When the stipends were due, the problem came to a head. We decided to work all day, pray, and meet at the end of the day. At 4:30, we met about our financial situation and started discussing the unpleasant options. At 4:45, the mail came. There was a $10,000 donation in the mail. At 4:46, we were humbled and in awe. With a sense of reserve and joy, we adjourned the meeting.

    God has provided for this ministry for five years. He has given us no excuse to merely count our blessings or circle our wagons. It is necessary to be careful and prudent, but these virtues must be informed by faith or the devil will slow all good intentions to a crawl. "If there is an award to be given for patience, it should be given to the devil. He has a lot of patience" (Mother Teresa). We are lacking in faith, hope, and love when we drag our feet while following Christ. So we are going ahead with the new house and praying that God will support it.

    Trusting in God is not all prosperity and roses. Jesus is the Prince of Peace, but He walked into the Temple, overturned the tables, and made chaos with a corded whip. He also stirs the mess in our souls. A contractor we know is a convert and former heavyweight pro boxer. I asked if he was interested in doing missionary work. He meekly declined. He said that too many evangelists pretend that Jesus will solve all of your problems, but his own experience is that problems seemed to only begin with meeting Jesus.

    Jesus does not really make chaos or problems. He stirs up existing problems and makes us aware of the false peace we strike with the world. Jesus ruins this false peace and gives us peace grounded on truth.

    We work alongside many government programs and secular charities. Lowering the crime rate and raising the graduation rate are worthy goals for a government agency and a secular charity, but these are not our ends. The human is our end, and we are trying to engage each human with love. This love goes beyond material assistance and running programs. It should be a mirror of God's love which provides for us and has particular interest in each of us.

    God wants much more for us than material goods and good health. Some people have suffered many worldly misfortunes, but they overflow with supernatural blessings. They may be disabled or destitute, but they radiate grace. This proves that God's love is more than worldly blessings. The most radical demonstration of this is Jesus on the cross.

It is the peculiar job of Christians to spread the Kingdom of God and infuse the whole world with His grace. The science of social work is not the science of Christian charity, and secular programs are not designed to bring God's grace into the world. Material goods and social services do not bring God's grace by themselves. "It is very important that the Church's charitable activity maintains all of its splendor and does not become just another form of social assistance" (Pope Benedict XVI). When Christians settle for merely providing a natural or material good, they are selling their mission and their life short.

To answer the Christian call of charity, men and women were appointed as deacons in the New Testament. Deacons were spiritual workers who brought material aid and Christ's love to the poor. It is only through love that conversion is possible, and it is only through love and conversion that amazing transformations are possible.

St. Stephen was one of the first seven deacons and the first martyr of the Church. His strong foundation in the faith is clear from his speech before being stoned to death (Acts 7:1–51). Like St. Stephen, St. James was deeply convicted of the link between Christianity and charity. As one of the twelve original apostles and the first bishop of Jerusalem, he wrote, "Religion that is pure and undefiled before God and the Father is this: to visit orphans and widows in their affliction, and to keep oneself unstained by the world" (Jas 1:27). The new house in Kansas City will be under the patronage of these two saints and will be called A Simple House of Sts. Stephen and James.

Thank you for being a blessing to us.

Clark Massey

GENTLENESS AND LETTING GO

Dear Friends and Family,   Fall 2008

Exciting news from A Simple House! In August, six new full-time volunteers joined our efforts. I live in a house packed with six women, and four men live in our Southeast house. In January, we are expanding to Kansas City, Missouri, where one of our donors has already generously bought us a house.

We have grown as a ministry and have been receiving encouragement from our friends and from God. It is affirming to our mission and adds to the excitement of going to Kansas City. Amidst this excitement, I am approaching the fourth year of my time at A Simple House. I face the new challenges that come with constancy and with deepened relationships. The difficult relationships are no longer the awkward new ones (there have been plenty of those to practice), but the ones that have developed since I've been here. Recently, I've needed to learn about letting go of control and when to be gentle with myself and others.

Sometimes, we can feel our unworthiness very acutely. We can feel our failings so deeply that we forget that it is part of the human experience to be flawed, and that Christ came just for that reason. We start thinking "Oh, everything would just be better if only I had done this, or not done that, or I was smarter, or prettier, or thinner, or <insert lacking quality here>, or just better!" It is amazing how when we are down, we can beat ourselves up even more! We tell ourselves to just be better and try harder. But this isn't what Christ came to do, nor is it what God is trying to tell us. When we begin to dwell on our failings, we can fall into two great lies: that God is not loving enough and that things would be better if we had more control (and God had less). There are moments for getting tough, but we cannot forget that there are times that we are so fragile that we need tenderness and support.

The poor in a special way need our gentleness. Their failings are ever-present. Dingy homes, broken furniture, need for food stamps, and the terrible school system can be constant reminders of failure. When we come to the poor, we have to remember that they may already feel inadequate. We see this often when we invite a mom to church. She will say that she wants to come to church but she has to take care of a few things like getting her family some church clothes, starting to live right, and kicking old habits. By these standards, we would not go to church either. When we can so clearly see all the things that are wrong in the lives of the poor, it can be tempting to "get tough" and start prescribing all of our solutions. Tough love can overlook that people are often in rough situations precisely because they are so fragile.

This summer, we worked hard to get Rhonda into a good Catholic school. The school program seemed competitive and faith-filled, and it was designed to accommodate low-income students. The school required business attire and had a "business boot camp" to prepare the students for the professional job placements they would have throughout the school year. Everything sounded top-notch. With great enthusiasm, I went out with Rhonda to buy her suits and dress shirts. We bought a cute purse to match and some school supplies. But with the start of boot camp came complaints about everything that could possibly be wrong with the school. I couldn't believe it. This was a once-in-a-lifetime opportunity, and she was hesitating. I called her mother one night to find out that Rhonda refused to go to school the next day. I tried talking to Rhonda, and I came down hard! What was she thinking, I wondered (and may have said). I told Rhonda that none of her reasons were sufficient. I was upset that Rhonda's mother wasn't "making" her go. The conversation ended after an hour. It didn't feel great but I was sure I was justified in all I said.

  I cannot begin to describe how angry I was. I was so mad that I could not recognize that Rhonda would still need all the support we could give her no matter what school she chose. I have known Rhonda since she was eleven, and I care about her deeply. I want things to be great for her. I want her to have all the best in life. She is a smart girl. I wanted things just perfect, and I thought I knew better than anyone how to get that for her. I was so caught up in trying to manage her life that I could not see that this Catholic school would be a bigger challenge than Rhonda was prepared to handle, and this was only academically. In coming down so hard on Rhonda and her mother, I was not able to see these things. All the justification I had felt on the phone was really quite unimportant. In trying to control everything, I had not noticed that all along, Rhonda was not enthusiastic about going to this school. Rhonda and her mother were greatly hurt by my lack of understanding, and our once close-knit relationship suffered.

  We need to encourage ourselves and others to come to God. Fr. Adam Ryan, OSB, one of our board members, told us that "order is not a prerequisite for coming to God, but a consequence of it." Rather than trying some absurd and grueling plan of micromanagement, we need to firmly ground ourselves on God and let our lives unfold from the gifts he has to give us. When we are too tough or controlling we reject God's plans and deny his graces. We also treat ourselves and others badly. People can become new focuses to manage. When we are not firmly grounded in God we get in an endless cycle of setting controls so that our lives don't spin out of hand.

A funny reminder of the beauty of letting go came when I was giving a tour to a new volunteer. Right as I was telling him that we were in the worst neighborhood I knew of, the car began sputtering. Could this be? I had been watching for the gas light (unaware that some cars don't have them). The car was out of gas. We managed to keep our cool and went to the house of a family I know. What ensued was one of the nicest visits I've had with a pretty rough family. It was funny and humbling as they one-by-one came down the stairs to ask if that really happened and yelled out their suggestions. In the end, everything was more than fine. God not only fixed the situation but used it to help us create a special bond with the family. It gave the new volunteer a better introduction to our ministry than any tour would have provided.

Some other tidbits of news:
- Our good friend just gave birth to a beautiful baby girl. The doctors told her that she should walk to speed the labor along. So, she took a bus downtown and walked three miles uphill to the hospital. She had the baby a few hours later.

- Thanks to the generous financial and legal help of our donors, the fifteen person Williams family will not be evicted and homeless. We have yet to find them adequate housing.

I hope this letter finds you all well. Your support and encouragement have been extremely valuable. Please keep praying for our ministry and our friends whom we serve.

With love,

Laura Cartagena

BEAUTY WILL SAVE THE WORLD

Dear Friends and Family,   Thanksgiving 2008

The four Bates sisters grew up with periods of homelessness and despair. Their mother is a pleasant person, but she struggles with drug abuse. During the bad times, there was no food, no lights, no gas, and strangers hung around their home. Because they benefited from government housing assistance, a social worker made an annual inspection of their home.

A few years ago, a social worker inspected the home while the utilities were cut off and revoked their housing assistance. The oldest sister was in her early twenties, the second oldest was graduating high school, and the twins were in the middle of high school.

Instead of becoming homeless, the sisters banded together to rent an apartment and finish their education. The oldest began braiding hair at a salon, and the second oldest took temporary jobs and was finally hired as a government contractor. The twins worked throughout high school and will graduate this year. The four sisters created a stable home for themselves with their own income. This inspiring achievement shows an incredible amount of courage and strength, but the real beauty of their lives was shown by what happened this summer.

A few months ago, their mother went on a drug binge. She was walking on a road late at night and was struck by a passing car. She was thrown into the air, and the driver never stopped. After landing, she was struck by another driver. This driver stopped and tried to comfort her until the ambulance arrived. After being airlifted to the hospital, she was placed in intensive care for over a week. Her leg was amputated, and she lost almost all movement in one arm. While recovering in the hospital, her daughters were constantly by her side keeping her company and trying to ease her pain.

The sisters comforted their mother with joy and love. In fact, I have rarely seen such a happy family. It is beautiful. Now that the mother has been discharged, the sisters have moved her into their home and take turns caring for her. The care they give their mother is inspiring because they are not bitter or self-righteous. Because of your support, our ministry has been able to help them with a few expenses and some food, but these sisters seem happy regardless of what happens.

Dostoyevsky and John Paul II believed that "beauty will save the world." The witness of the Bates sisters is not beautiful at a superficial level. It is a story of injustice, sin, and failed responsibilities, but this ugliness is transformed by the sisters' forgiveness, joy, and love. This beauty is not the beauty of a lily. It is the beauty of the crucifixion.

We fall in love with beautiful things, and God is the most beautiful. But to understand His beauty, we have to understand the beauty of the crucifixion. The witness of the Bates sisters has a similar beauty to the witness of the crucifixion, and when we stand in the presence of this beauty, we are ashamed. We are ashamed because of all the times we were unloving, unforgiving, merciless, or ungenerous. They shame us because they are bigger people than we are. They are bigger people not because of toughness or will power. They are bigger because of Christ's grace flowing through their humility, faith, and love.

Sin makes ugly. God makes beautiful. A favorite saying amongst the people we serve is, "God don't like ugly." I once corrected a woman by saying, "God loves ugly people too." She told me that I had missed the point, and she completed the saying, "God don't like ugly. God don't like pretty. God likes righteous and holy." Sometimes I wonder, "Who is the real missionary here?"

The goal of Christian missionary work is not to make people adopt a set of ideas like a Republican or Democrat trying to grow their party. Although beliefs and dogmas are necessary to keep religion from becoming a game of make-believe, they are not enough for salvation. Even the devil knows dogma, but he does not understand the beauty of God.

The goal of missionary work is to demonstrate God's beauty and help people to fall in love with Him. When religion is reduced to merely a set of ideas, it is no longer the relationship where we give ourselves to God. It becomes a self-justification project. Justification goes by many names (legalism, pride, proselytizing . . .), and it is the enemy of true religion. We must become like little children in order to enter the kingdom of Heaven. We should not aspire to the knowledge of a child but to the love and humility of a child.

Gemel Lamont Williams was murdered. Our ministry has known Gemel for over three years. We have visited with him, prayed with him, and helped him out when possible. Gemel was 27 years old and prayed with our missionaries the day he died. Please pray for him, and thank you for making this ministry possible.

Thank you for being a blessing to this ministry.

Clark Massey

LEAVING DC

Dear Friends and Family,   Christmas 2008

The new staffs of the Kansas City and DC houses have been decided. Volunteers opening the Kansas City house include: Jim, Heather, Sylvia, Kelly, Jessica, and myself. The staff of DC includes: Ryan H., Ryan F., Laura, and Bianca. After the decision was made, the Kansas City volunteers had to talk with families about the move. I will be leaving some families that I've known for almost five years.

This parting is especially difficult because the neighborhoods we evangelize are full of failed responsibilities and inconstancy. Parents often make promises to their children and fail to keep them, and according to the US Census, over 98% of the neighborhood families are led by single mothers. It is not unusual for a child to have only met their father once or twice. Because of these problems and the intense pain and disappointment they create, Simple House volunteers have always been careful with commitments. During training, it is constantly taught: <u>always under-promise and over-deliver.</u>

Good friendships make leaving painful. One of my deepest friendships has been with a family who joined the Church with me and Laura as godparents. This is the closest I've ever been to being a parent, and last year, I spent my mornings driving the kids to school. Being a parent is hard work! After worrying with the family, helping them, and trying to keep my promises, I had to sit down and tell them that I'm going to Kansas City. While I told six kids and their mom that I was leaving, snot and tears made tracks down my face. I cannot remember ever being this emotional. The kids stared at me and wondered what all of this meant. During the meeting, I made some commitments to them. I would visit on certain dates, and we planned a summer road trip. May God allow Simple House and me to fulfill these commitments. May God give us more friendships like this.

In another family, they took the news with prolonged silence. The conversation went in different directions, but leaving came up every fifteen minutes. Their mother was one of the first people to welcome Simple House into the neighborhood, and she died suddenly about four years ago. She left behind a 31 year-old daughter and a 19 year-old son. Each year, her children hold a vigil on the anniversary of her death.

The vigils are a gathering of tough looking young men holding candles, praying, and sharing memories. This is followed by a big meal of shrimp and potato stew. The first year of the vigil, I did not understand the significance of my role. I went to pay my respects about an hour after the vigil should have started. To my horror, they had been waiting for me to lead the prayer and no one would eat until I had the first bowl of stew.

Our ministry is the closest tie this family has to church, and although they have come to Mass a few times, they still consider our visits and group prayers an important part of their religious life. A few years ago, Laura and I left the event and she started laughing about the surreal situation. She and I are missionaries raised in the suburbs, and a group of inner-city men treat us as honored guests at their solemn vigil. This part of the ministry is an unplanned and unexpected gift from God.

Simple House volunteers are hoping for a big Christmas. Besides Christmas bags, presents, and Christmas dinners, there will be another interesting Christmas outreach. A few years ago, A Simple House hosted a dinner and speaker to a mixed audience of donors, volunteers, and families. We had a long relationship with one of the families that was staying at a homeless shelter. The family excused themselves early in order to make the shelter's curfew. Everyone found the talk edifying, but the family leaving early was downstairs stealing money, checks, and credit cards from coats on the coat tree. As people left, the theft was discovered. Laura and I went to the homeless shelter, and the family had not made curfew. They were on a spending spree.
    Drug addiction and greed were too much of a temptation for them. We did our best to hold the family responsible, but our relationship has never fully healed. This Christmas the family is in great need, and instead of helping them with presents, Ryan F. and Jim are going to help them in a nontraditional way. The family's oldest son has been in prison for over three years a few hours outside the city. He has not seen anyone from his family in all that time because they are too poor to travel and visit him. Ryan and Jim are arranging a road trip to reunite the family for a day before Christmas.

    There are so many unknowns and moving parts related to the survival and success of this work, the only logical response is prayer. Instead of being logical, I worry and grasp for material solutions and control. Please pray for us. May God always provide as He always has. God did provide, God can provide, and God will provide.

Merry Christmas and may Christ's peace be with you.
Clark Massey

FASTING

Dear Friends and Family,   Easter 2009

    We have been working hard in DC. Now that Clark is in Kansas City, Ryan and I are learning a lot about running the ministry. We have been blessed with many new volunteers and seminarians. For Easter, we gave baskets to 150 moms and 400 kids.

    I've known Claudia since she was eleven and our relationship with her family has had ups and downs. Claudia is now sixteen and having her second baby. Claudia's life has been difficult, and her challenges will increase with motherhood. We recently helped throw her a baby shower.

    When we arrived, Bianca and I were met with excitement and put to work preparing and arranging food. The music, commotion, games, and soul food made a good party. As I looked around, I became misty eyed. It was an honor to be present at this moment. The circumstances of Claudia's pregnancy were not perfect, and nobody at the party was perfect. A family which is not always "together" was coming together in an extraordinary way to celebrate motherhood and new life. Her family and friends honored the occasion with dignity and joy. Amidst all this, I was put to work as if I was part of the family while simultaneously being treated as a guest of honor. There was something very humbling about the whole situation.

In February, we went on a weeklong retreat. The Beachner family hosted us on a beautiful property with fields, woods, and a big lake in southeastern Kansas. It was a great setting for exploration and reflection. We read the Catechism on prayer and studied the Gospel of Luke with a focus on how Jesus ministered. Our days were spent in silence except for our nightly discussions on the reading. At the end of the week, we celebrated with the Beachners and roasted a pig. The retreat was a great preparation for Lent.

I am finally beginning to grasp the beauty of fasting. At the start of Lent, my spiritual director said, "If you are going to fast, you need to feast on something else." My prayer life grew as I fasted from snacking and asked God to be my sustenance. Instead of challenging and frustrating, this Lent was comforting and exciting.

Sacrifice is not for its own sake, but a preparation for something greater. Catholics are sometimes accused of doing penance because we like suffering or are trying to earn salvation. It is easy to believe these accusations when we practice our Lenten observances as a set of weird rules. Instead, Lent is meant to open us to God's joy and peace. My sacrifices were small compared to the joy I received. I couldn't have earned it! My sacrifices clear the clutter and get me out of God's way.

Your generosity makes our mission possible. This mission has recently become more public. *The Washington Post Magazine* featured A Simple House as its cover story. Senator Sam Brownback invited us to meet with him at his office, and we are looking forward to him visiting our ministry. In addition, a number of schools and churches invited us to give talks to their youth.

With love,
Laura Cartagena

GEORGE'S STORY

Dear Friends and Family,   Easter 2009

    Easter was cold and rainy. After we finished our outreach in the projects, we brought chocolate bunnies, hot drinks, and Burger King gift cards to a few guys living underneath a bridge. Despite the brutal Kansas City winters, they never sleep inside. George was the only one there. We had been friends with George for a few weeks, and we were hoping that he would come to our house for Easter dinner. He is an alcoholic, and he drinks 30 beers a day to not feel sick. When we arrived, George was wet, cold, inconsolable, and barely coherent. He had been vomiting blood for a few days and was groveling to be taken to detox.

    Death by hypothermia was a real threat. George needed to go to an emergency room, but if we called an ambulance, the police would come too. The men living under the bridge would feel betrayed and lose their belongings if the police came. So we started the long coaxing process to get George to our car.

    His grief at his friendless and desperate state was terrible. If emotion and desire could cure alcoholism, George would not have a problem. He desperately wants friends and not to be a "dysfunctional" human. Our urgings and long negotiations wandered between joking, threatening an ambulance, talking about his kids, and his threats of suicide.

    During the strange exchange, I struggled to find the right words. I asked if he was raised Christian. He laughed and cried. My naïve question was interpreted as,

"Do you know God?" As such, it was asking a man who talks, resists, begs, pleads, and argues with God in his hardship if he "knew God." The question was ridiculous to him, and his crying and laughing made this obvious.

When Sylvia pulled the van up to the bridge, we got George into the van and started driving to the hospital. An undercover cop, who we now realized had been watching the situation develop, followed us to the hospital. This became especially nerve racking when George decided to have one more beer before detox.

George stayed at the hospital until his immediate sickness subsided, and he left before his vomiting was treated. He is now seeing a doctor to help with the vomiting, but he has not made it to detox. George did not get under the bridge by one day of bad choices, and he isn't going to leave the bridge after one day of good choices. Nothing as simple as a job, an apartment, or a chocolate bunny will solve his problems. George needs love, friends, and God. Even if he never fully "gets better" or becomes "functional," his life is of infinite value.

Our first Kansas City outreach was a success. The families in the projects have warmly welcomed our presence, and we need to fully open the food pantry and mothers' closet. $700 a month gives groceries to 30+ families and about $250 a month allows us to help mothers with diapers and baby supplies. Our food deliveries provide a great relief and witness, but summer is the hardest time to find food and cash donations. Please help us help the poor.

Thank you for supporting this mission.

Clark Massey

GEORGE'S STORY, PART 2

Dear Friends and Family,   Summer 2009

    The Easter newsletter told the story of our friend George and how we found him underneath a bridge vomiting blood and delirious. We took him to a hospital, and after a brief stay, he skipped detox and went back to the bridge.

    Recently, Sylvia and I met George at the public library after he had finished begging for beer money. We were going to take him out to lunch, but he pleaded with us to take him to his hometown two hours away. His brother-in-law had just passed away, and he wanted to attend the viewing. George was intoxicated and in a lot of emotional pain. He wanted to drink even more.

    As George went to buy a 30-pack of beer, Sylvia and I talked about taking him to the viewing. George would need a chance to shower, shave, and change clothes. Instead of lunch, we told George that he would be picked up in an hour to clean up, and we went to Walmart for supplies. He promised not to drink at our house or on the way to the viewing.

    While we were gone, George went back to the bridge to use a friend's cell phone and hide his belongings. He called his family and told them he was coming. A group of 20 Christian students showed up under the bridge while he was getting ready to leave. They prayed over him and gave him $5 for gas money. When we arrived, George was encouraged but still drunk. He gave me the gas money and rode to our house to clean up. During the process of cleaning up and the two-hour drive to the viewing, he was sobering up.

On the long drive, we heard a lot about George's life and how proud he was of his children. It was beautiful to hear him talk about his family. He hated staying with them, but he loved the fact that they wanted him. He warned us, "I may be getting kidnapped when I get there!" He begged us not to leave town without him unless he decided to stay. He didn't want us to cooperate with a kidnapping.

He analyzed the situation like this: "If I stay under the bridge, I have freedom, beer, and drugs. If I stay with my kids, it's like I'm in jail. It's like they are the adults and I am the kid." He said this with a mildly ironic tone. He knew that his "jailors" loved him and that his wonderful grandkids were in the "jail" too.

Halfway to his hometown, we stopped for gas. The gas station cashier recognized George from many years before and gave him a hug. As we got back into the car, George was amazed at everything that had happened that day, and he kept repeating, "Tell me Jesus ain't alive!"

When we arrived at the funeral home, George's homecoming was at least as important as the viewing. He was greeted by a swarm of his children and grandchildren. His children were choked up, and they thanked us with tears. While the family talked, Sylvia and I wandered around the deserted town square.

After about an hour, we saw George walking across the town square with five young grandchildren running around him. He was coming to tell us he wanted to stay home. At the time of this letter, George is still at home and sober. We promised to visit him during August to go fishing.

George's decision was between his family and a bridge, between true and false happiness. Despite the clear correct answer, it was hard for him to make the right decision. His children know that their father's struggle with addiction will be continual without a divine miracle, but for now, it is time to celebrate. Many prayers were answered, and there is one less man living and drinking under a bridge.

Everyone makes daily decisions between sinful desires (false happiness) and following Christ (true happiness). Christians are called to teach humanity the way to life and the way to live. This teaching should not always be a lecture on morality. The witness of true fun, happiness, and joy allows people to see beyond sin, and it demonstrates the rewards of life with Christ. This witness teaches people how to live.

Our DC houses are thriving under the direction of Ryan and Laura. Please continue to pray for Mrs. Williams and her 13 children. Despite the heroic effort of her pro bono attorneys, they were evicted for breaking the terms of her settlement. Their quest for housing took them all the way to West Virginia and back. The family is now split up and living with friends in the DC area. The Simple House volunteers have been with the family along the way and will continue to help.

Please pray for the healing of the Smith family in DC. The mother was recently shot. The older sons are living the street life or in jail, and the younger sons had a gun accident. Faith, hope, and love are needed. Please pray.

Your generosity makes our ministry possible. Thank you for donations and prayers!

Clark Massey

RACHEL'S STORY

Dear Friends and Family,   Thanksgiving 2009

    This May I graduated with a degree in electrical engineering. When I started college, I went into electrical engineering with the intention of using it for mission work and to help people in poor countries. As school went on, I began to realize that true mission work is more than just helping people by giving them things. I realized that really helping someone involves getting to know them, loving them, spending time with them, and ultimately bringing them closer to God.

    When I began my search for an organization to volunteer with after college, I had two conditions. I wanted to use electrical engineering to help people, and I wanted the organization to be Catholic. When I couldn't find something that fit my criteria, I focused on finding a Catholic volunteer organization. A friend of mine told me about an inner-city mission in Washington, DC, that he had volunteered with. I found that it was a Catholic mission group that took faith and prayer seriously, and it focused on forming relationships with people rather than just doing things for them.

    Since I joined the Kansas City location of A Simple House, I've learned how to mud drywall, stain a floor, use a map, function without the Internet, drive in a big city, paint little kids' faces, and lead a book club meeting. Soon I'll be driving in snow and keeping myself warm during a "real" non-Louisiana winter.

    Besides all the practical things I've learned, I've been challenged to pray more than I ever thought was possible or necessary. I'm learning to wake up in the morning to pray (step one: going to bed on time), to read spiritual reading and theology, and to read the Bible every day. I'm figuring out how to develop relationships with people and even to pray with people I don't know very well. I'm also discovering what the ministry of Simple House means.

    There's a homeless lady we know named Rachel. One day, my ministry partner told me that we had to go looking for Rachel. I had no idea what that meant, but I went along with it. We went to a flower shop, where we found Rachel's shopping cart in the parking lot, but no Rachel. Then we went to a women's day shelter and a Catholic Worker house, but there was no sign of her. So we went back to the flower shop and left a note in her shopping cart. The note invited her to our house the next day for her birthday.
    Since then, we've brought her coffee, had lunch, and talked with her several times. We bring her to our house sometimes to shower and wash her clothes. I'm not sure why she's homeless, but it seems like she has lived this way awhile. As we got to know her more, we decided to try to get her into some sort of housing before winter.
    We weren't sure she would go for the housing idea because she generally distrusts people and the government, and she won't stay in shelters. We had set a date with her to visit the art museum. (It's free and Rachel likes history so we thought she might like it.) It was a great day. She told us about her family and about her sister who lives in Iowa where they were born. As the conversation went on, we finally asked if she would like us to help her get housing, and surprisingly, she went for it right away.

When we started looking for housing, we found out Rachel doesn't have any form of identification. Our first step was to try to get a government ID for her, which is hard to do when you don't have any documents saying who you are. We invited her over for lunch and a haircut, and we were going to call her sister to help us get Rachel's birth certificate. As we sat down to make the call, Rachel said she had something to tell us. She said her name might not actually be Rachel. Then she launched into a long explanation about how she may have been kidnapped, and the memory she has of her childhood probably isn't her real memory, all while weaving several conspiracy theories into the whole conversation. Our already complex task suddenly exploded into figuring out how to get housing for someone with no ID who wasn't even sure of her real name. There was nothing else we could do that day to work on housing, so we played Yahtzee instead.

We haven't given up on finding housing for Rachel, but as this task becomes more impossible, our need for God's grace and providence becomes more obvious. Last winter, she lived under a pile of blankets on the threshold of an abandoned building. We may not be able to get Rachel a home this winter, but we'll continue to work with her, spend time with her, and love her.

I'll be with A Simple House at least until May. It has been a really great but very difficult experience. I would appreciate your prayers.

Love,

Danielle Howard

THE JACKSONS' VERY BAD DAY

Dear Friends and Family,   Christmas 2009

People often ask me what I do. I usually give a weak answer instead of being gutsy and saying, "I'm trying to imitate Jesus." So what does Jesus do? Jesus is a carpenter and "the savior of the world" (Jn 4:42). He saves the world through love.

Saving the world with love is different than saving the world with science or with stuff. Jesus could have arrived with a heavenly dump truck full of things. Instead, He arrived as an infant, and He left us still wanting and working on our problems.

There is a Christian principle called "subsidiarity." The idea is that people should do what they can for themselves, and if you take away their responsibilities by doing too many things for them, you hurt them. Nevertheless, not everyone is able to manage all of their needs and responsibilities. Mental illness, misfortune, temptation, and injustice can interfere with someone doing what they need to do. In addition, people can find themselves in a hole too deep to climb out of alone. When someone can't fulfill their responsibilities or they have gotten into a deep hole, friendship and love is Jesus' response—the Christian response.

Everyone needs love, and no one can make or earn love for themselves. Love must be given and received as a gift. The poor and the wealthy alike need love, and the needs of the poor and the blessings of the wealthy create an opportunity for authentic love. Realizing this opportunity is the work of A Simple House.

The Jackson family is poor. They are six adults and ten children living in a three bedroom house. They recently moved into the house by pushing a shopping cart and a broken SUV from their old house. After they arrived, they discovered a gas leak. The landlord did not fix the leak, and they had to turn off the gas. Without gas, they shower with cold water, and they use the oven and space heaters for heat. This inefficient heat made the electric bill sky high. When they gave a relative money to pay the bill, he took the money and moved out.

The leader of the house is a grandmother in her forties. She asked us to help them find a new place to live. When we arrived to help the grandmother, her brother was burning sticks and leaves in a grill to cook a warm meal.

As we visited houses with the grandmother and her daughters, they received a call from home. A water pipe had burst in the basement. To make matters worse, someone broke into our car and stole one of their purses. The woman lost her ID, seven children's social security cards, and a food stamp card. Despite the catastrophic day, the three women were in surprisingly good spirits. We did not fulfill all of their needs, but they were thankful and upbeat about the help and friendship.

When we left them that night, I thought that some of the people staying in the house would go somewhere else for the night. Despite the conditions, no one left. They had nowhere else to go.

Some days the members of the Jackson family seem like victims, other days they seem to be at fault, and most days they seem like survivors. The truth includes all of these things. The real issue is not how to assign credit or blame (that is a judgment for God); the real issue is how to love.

Pope Benedict's new encyclical, *Love in Truth*, is a play on the biblical words "truth in love" (Eph 4:15). Loving the poor, and even our families, in truth means not being guided by oversimplifications. A simplification like "the poor are always victims" is abused to create an emotional response, and "the poor are always at fault" is abused to excuse inaction. Neither of these approaches gives dignity to the poor. Loving in truth means asking the straightforward question, "What is the best way to help?"

The Jackson family's situation sounds like a problem that needs a lot of money to solve, but I don't think this is the case. The Jackson family needs someone to work with them, give them rides, love them, fix a few emergencies, and shield the children from some of the harm. We want to move them into a new home by Christmas. We also want to make sure that the children have shoes, coats, food, and indestructible toys for a happy Christmas. Your generosity makes this possible. Ms. Jackson and all of us owe you a tremendous thank you.

Christmas Plans

Before the Christmas season is over, you will hear at least a dozen rants about how consumerism is ruining Christmas and how stuff gets in the way of "the Christmas spirit." All of this talk puts presents at odds with love.

Presents are supposed to embody love. I love getting and giving presents! I think that is part of the reason God made A Simple House. He gave me a job where I get to give a lot of presents. A Simple House is trying to give Christmas presents to 182 children and Christmas baskets to 250 needy families. We need help to make this possible.

Thank you and Merry Christmas,

Clark Massey

DIFFICULT MINISTRY

Dear Friends and Family,   Lent 2010

    When I met Terri five years ago, she was fragile, too thin, and her eyes were bulging. She was sick and not taking care of herself. At that time, Terri lived in one of the worst project neighborhoods in DC, and her apartment felt like a cave. She was waiting to die. With encouragement and help, she has recovered, but she has had to face many new challenges.

    Terri is unique, scatterbrained, and often difficult. Even after her recovery, I never felt like visiting Terri. Her phone calls were pushy and annoying. Sometimes there would be several messages on the answering machine with Terri yelling at us. Terri would make unreasonable demands and try to guilt us if we did not meet them. She accused us of being selfish and unchristian. After a while, I harbored resentment and frustration. I stopped bringing a message of hope to Terri. Rather, I judged her and focused on her flaws. I had gradually become hardened to her. Subconsciously, I had written Terri off as a lost cause.

    In the fall, I visited Terri with a part-time volunteer. I planned on quickly dropping off groceries before visiting a different family. Instead, I had a long conversation with Terri. Before I knew what I was saying, I committed to a weekly Bible study with her. This was the last thing I wanted to do. To my surprise, she was eager to learn more about Christianity. She even asked for homework assignments each week.

We started visiting her weekly with a Bible study, homework assignment, and a box of cookies. I started looking forward to seeing Terri. Beyond edifying Bible studies, I enjoyed her company and her family. Our withering relationship started becoming a friendship again. I had forgotten how funny and caring she can be.

Terri's life is chaotic and difficult. She has been through long periods of homelessness and lived in the worst neighborhoods of the city. She has lived the street life, and she is still tempted by it. Consequently, Terri's children have been through many trials and still have problems.

Her oldest son is in prison. The only time I met him he was wearing a bulletproof vest in his own home. He knew people were after him. The dispute was related to drugs, or a woman, or both. At the time, he was a suspect in a drive-by shooting that hit another young man we knew. He often calls Terri from prison to hear a loving voice and receive moral support.

Terri's two oldest daughters became mothers in their mid-teens, and they have been raising their kids in Terri's house. Terri's oldest girl is pregnant again and avoiding her. She has not been home for months and has abandoned her son. Terri's five-year-old grandson often wakes up from nightmares and cries for his mother. Terri is trying to find her daughter, and she may try to get custody of her grandson. In the meantime, she has to provide for and comfort her grandson.

Terri is closest to her youngest son, Henry. He is fourteen years old, and he is always polite, although sometimes high, when we see him. He has been locked up in group homes and rehab for the last two years. He was recently arrested for stealing a car. Car theft and joyriding are common crimes in DC. When Henry was ten, we had to take Terri to pick him up from jail in the middle of the night. Henry had been hanging out with older boys who stole a car, and someone called the police when they saw Henry jump out of the moving vehicle. Terri has been going to all of Henry's court hearings. She misses him and wants to give him the support he needs. Even though the judge may not let him come home, she has been arranging for tutors and enrolling Henry in every program she thinks might help him. She wants him home, but as a ward of the state, he may receive more discipline and guidance than at home. Terri prays that the judge will decide whatever is best for Henry.

    Terri's youngest daughter does not fit in with the rest of her family. Terri's mother raised the youngest daughter by sending her to Bible camps and keeping her active in church. Her mother passed away in 2007, and Terri's daughter lives with her now. This daughter has little in common with her siblings, and Terri has a hard time figuring out how to relate to her. Although she is staying out of trouble, Terri worries about her. Terri may lose her if she does not receive enough attention, but the needs of Terri's other children always seem so pressing to her.

    You may remember a story we wrote in a letter in 2006. A priest was speaking at our house, and we invited some donors and people to whom we minister. One of the women we invited brought her family along with another family we did not know. Towards the end of the night they made an abrupt exit, looted the coat rack, and walked out with five or six credit cards belonging to our guests. This woman was Terri.

    Terri is still sometimes difficult and demanding. It is easy to write off a person like Terri, but she and God have surprised me. God continues to love us no matter how difficult we are and no matter what we do wrong. There is hope for all of us.

The Kansas City volunteers have a new housemate named Rachel. Last winter, Rachel was homeless and slept outside every night. They started a relationship with her and gained her confidence by bringing her coffee each morning.

At the DC house, Lucy has shown a surprising improvement in mental and physical health.

I am grateful for all of you.
With love,

Laura Cartagena

NEW EVANGELIZATION

Dear Friends and Family,   Easter 2010

The first "Friends and Family" letter was mailed in 2003. Because of the generous response, I moved to Anacostia and started the ministry. In December 2005, the Kirwan Catholic Worker donated a house in Northwest DC, and in 2008, a donor provided a duplex for volunteers in Kansas City.

There are two formerly homeless women living in the houses, and 16 full-time volunteers have lived and served in the houses. There have also been many part-time volunteers including 17 seminarians. Thank you and God for these blessings. It is an honor to serve the poor and receive so much encouragement and support from donors.

A Simple House feeds, serves, and supports an impressive number of people, but there is no statistical data that can really explain the work. A Simple House is best understood as a response to scripture and a few modern problems. Although we have grown, we need to always recommit to our call.

Spiritual Poverty

There is persistent poverty in America. This poverty has survived multibillion dollar fixes and the Great Society programs of the sixties. A former member of the Kennedy administration said that the remaining poverty is "a problem which defies a solution," and there is a saying in Southeast DC that goes, "The government declared war on poverty, and poverty won."

Shelter, food, and treatment for addiction are often available in American cities, but something mysterious prevents people from taking advantage of them. Many people have lost hope, and this loss of hope causes behaviors that resemble a slow suicide. To provide material goods without friendship or spiritual support only continues the problem. The real problem is spiritual poverty.

A Simple House is a basic response to this poverty. Homelessness, parents abandoning their children, severe depression, drug addiction, hunger, and young children missing school are frequent problems in the families we serve. Our work involves gaining their trust, providing material support, and helping the parents grow. This type of work is always unique. It has involved sheltering families, Bible studies, providing for neglected children, and encouraging mothers who are depressed.

Friendship Evangelization

Man's ego can turn spirituality into a weapon. This usually happens through proselytizing, which is condemned by Jesus (Mt 23:15). It is also true that someone can proselytize with secularism in a way that is violent and cruel. Real Christian evangelization and charity are as kind as they are radical. They facilitate a relationship with God and are only secondarily concerned with promoting a set of ideas.

All evangelization must integrate charity. The charity that addresses people's deepest needs must be guided by truth. Unfortunately, evangelization and charity are usually seen as separate activities. The work of A Simple House is a reintegration of evangelization and charity. This means preaching truth with love and loving in truth.

"So deeply do we care for you that we are determined to share with you not only the gospel of God but also our own selves, because you have become very dear to us." (1 Thess. 2:8)

Friendship evangelization was the first evangelization, and it is the new evangelization. As we become intimate friends with Christ, it feels natural to introduce other friends to Him. If Christ is not a friend, the evangelist is talking about someone they do not know and an awkwardness results. Friendship evangelization does not try to argue someone into the Church. It strives to love them into the Church, and it meets their spiritual and material needs. Friendship evangelization is the method of our work.

Reliance on Divine Providence

Jesus said, "If you wish to be perfect, go, sell what you have and give to the poor, and you will have treasure in heaven. Then come, follow me" (Mt 19:21). He also said, "Take nothing for your journey, neither a staff, nor a bag, nor bread, nor money; and do not even have two tunics apiece" (Lk 9:3).

A Simple House has renounced endowments and has no more than three months operating expenses at any time. Because of this, there are times of feasting and times of fasting at A Simple House. During the feasts, we provide for the poor with a super abundance, and during the fasts, we deny ourselves and serve the poor as best we can.

This way of living gets the most out of every donation, and it teaches volunteers to depend upon God for their daily bread. St. Paul said, "I have learned to be content in whatever circumstances I am. I know how to get along with humble means, and I also know how to live in prosperity; in any and every circumstance I have learned the secret of being filled and going hungry, both of having abundance and suffering need. I can do all things through Him who strengthens me" (Phil 4:11-13).

The gifts given to A Simple House are never hoarded, and because of our voluntary poverty, the overhead costs are minimal.

We only have **12** days of operating funds.

A Simple House is an experiment in Christianity, and its survival is a miracle. There are no specially trained professionals or special programs to inspire faith or hope. There has only been love, and love has borne great fruit. Please pray for us and support our work.

Thank you.

Clark Massey

GOD AND FUN

Dear Friends and Family,   Summer 2010

    I have played the bass guitar in a rock band for over two years. One night, I left a gig early because I had to take a family to church the next morning. As I said goodbye to my friends, a woman asked me, "Are you really going to choose God over fun?" I sputtered out an unconvincing "yes" and made for the door. That question hit me hard, waking me up to a growing tension in my life. The band was becoming more successful, and at the same time, I was gaining more responsibilities at A Simple House.

    There was a conflict between my goals and aspirations. I was continually sacrificing one commitment for the other, trying to move forward in two different directions. By doing both, I was not choosing either one fully. Anxiety, stress, and fatigue set in from helping the poor by day and pursuing rock stardom by night.

    I decided to make a retreat in order to think clearly, de-stress, and gain some perspective. A friend generously offered to let me camp in the woods on his property, and I jumped at the chance. I must have been really stressed out because I don't even like camping! But what began as a relaxing change of scenery turned into some tough soul searching. Where was my life headed? All of a sudden, it was decision time.

    When Jesus invited the rich young man to give up his possessions and follow Him, he walked away sad. He didn't have the courage to accept the invitation. I imagine he felt like I did – torn between the blessings I already have and a deeper commitment to God, with all its uncertainty. After all, why would God ask me to give up what He had given in the first place?

Perhaps the rich young man did not fully understand the invitation. The real choice is not between God and fun. Christian sacrifice has a purpose, and it is always for the sake of love. Every Christian sacrifice is an opportunity to go for broke on the greatest love of your life and your ultimate happiness. It is a bold choice against selfishness, for the good of another, and in favor of a rich relationship with God. Fundamentally, sacrifice is an act of trust. It requires trust that God is the author of our happiness, not us. This trust is the basis of a relationship with God and the doorway to true freedom and lasting happiness. This trust is faith.

Life is a series of recommitments and conversions to the Lord. Leaving the band and devoting myself more fully to A Simple House was one of the largest and most rewarding recommitments I have made. In a similar way, Clark asked all Simple House volunteers to join in making a "June 8th Resolution." It was a challenge for us to be a more spiritual ministry by paying more attention to prayer and reflection.

Ruth and Her Boys

Ruth's house is always cluttered. Her health problems and the special needs of her two adopted sons have always stood in the way of her keeping a clean home. Simple House volunteers have worked with the family for over three years, and we have cleaned and fixed up their home on multiple occasions. No matter how much we accomplish on these visits, the house is always refilled with garbage in only a few weeks. It is inconceivable to me that anyone could live this way day in and day out. The problem came to a head last winter when the house burned down during the worst snowstorm in DC history. One of her sons left a candle unattended amidst the mess. The fire spread quickly and destroyed the home. Fortunately, no one was hurt.

Ruth has a mix of problems, and it is difficult to tell the difference between her fault and misfortune. Yet Ruth never uses her problems as an excuse not to love. Since the house burned down, she has found a job, moved into a new house, and offered her home to a young man who goes by the name "Pain." (I know this seems like a wild punch-line, but that is his actual nickname.) Pain does not know his real mother and has been neglected and abused by his adoptive family.

To show his gratitude, Pain helps clean the house. He is also looking for a job and a way to attend college. Though Pain is the only one staying there, he is just one of many neighborhood boys who could call Ruth's house a second home. These young men are impressive. Like Ruth's sons, they are intelligent, polite, well-spoken, and eager to talk about their goals and interests.

This is a puzzling and beautiful situation. Why do these unique young men spend so much time at Ruth's home? Despite the mess, they find something in Ruth's home that they don't find on the streets or at their own homes. Ruth's flaws may be apparent, but her love is genuine. The boys overlook her deficiencies because she is generous with her time and affection. Ruth's problems are not obstacles to love. She loves despite her problems.

Sincerely,

Ryan Hehman

THE HIDDEN POOR

Dear Friends and Family, October 2010

Some people we serve are very vocal, and all of their problems seem like a crisis. The most vocal people we serve are not the neediest people because they are good at getting help. The "dropping of everything" to meet an exaggerated crisis leads to less ministry, and it makes us ignore real need that is often hidden.

The hidden poor are the people who are not vocal. They have the greatest unmet needs because they don't bother other people. For example, we met a mother of six who was too depressed to leave her small apartment during daylight hours, and we found an old man in a wheelchair who lived on the top floor of a burnt out house. In a different way, we found a woman in plain view. She slept every winter night under blankets on the sidewalk, and she lied about why she didn't need help. All of these people have been helped by your generosity and by dedicated volunteers.

Working with the hidden poor requires some daring. We have to seek them out, realize there is a longing for help, and take a gentle initiative. They are downtrodden, and they usually have a heavy sadness of heart. Their situation somehow demands Jesus' beatitude "Blessed are the poor."

An interesting hidden person we recently met is 22 years old, homeless, and barely speaks. She sleeps underneath a bridge, but she has stayed away from the alcohol, drugs, and prostitution of the streets. She could go back home, but she refuses. We suspect that the reason she won't go home is the same reason she won't talk. We are trying to give her love and friendship with some help towards concrete ends. Shelter and a job at an understanding workplace are her most immediate needs. We are trying to find her a part-time job and open our house to her. Thank you for making this ministry possible.

A friend of ours left his family and job to live on the streets. After a night of drinking and arguments, his family brought him to a hospital when he threatened suicide. His grown children and Simple House volunteers signed affidavits to have him committed for four days at a mental hospital. This was a very strange time for A Simple House. Although we avoid giving help that may enable or harm someone, we almost never do something against the will of the person we are serving. These affidavits caused hard feelings and dramatic accusations. By the end of the 96-hour involuntary commitment, he forgave the affidavits and felt torn but thankful about the situation.

Two weeks after being released, he threatened suicide again, and Simple House volunteers had to search the streets for him and call 911. The situation was painful and manipulative. Lies about substance abuse and the previous suicide attempts that left scars across his wrists made it difficult to help. Our friend tried to fill his great need for healing with drugs and our friendship. We did not know how to respond, and it left everyone tragically worn out and dejected. Only God can fill this type of need.

Christians are susceptible to becoming pushovers and people pleasers while attributing their actions to love. This leads to many bad acts in the name of "helping" others. Enabling drug abusers is the most obvious example of this problem. The enabler is not trying to do wrong, but the help is misguided. The situation usually ends with less love and many confused feelings.

    The art of being a Christian is to have kind love while doing what is right. This art is usually pleasing to everyone even while it denies and changes their desires. A human's deepest desires are ordered toward the good, and this art of love makes men happy because it addresses these deep desires even if it contradicts whims. This art is not always successful. When it fails, the Christian should not take the affront personally because it is Christ being rejected.

    God is very pleasing, but He is not a people pleaser. God allows Himself to be abused, but He is not a pushover. Jesus was tortured and executed by the same people he came to help, but at the same time, His kindness and patience were complete. He did not lay a self-serving smackdown on guilty men. Instead He says, "Father forgive them because they do not know what they do" (Lk 23:34).

    Ryan and Laura are getting married! They have been full-time volunteers at A Simple House for over four years. Their wedding will have a large impact on our community and the ministry. Please pray for this transition.

Thank you,

Clark Massey

RACHEL'S STORY, PART 2

Dear Friends and Family, Thanksgiving 2010

    I met Rachel when I first came to Simple House last August. She lived on the porch of a soup kitchen and spent her days between a Catholic Worker house, a flower shop, and a women's day shelter. Simple House volunteers had met her the winter before, and they had gotten to know her by bringing her coffee and visiting with her. When I wrote last November, we had made an attempt to fill out paperwork for her birth certificate, but the attempt failed. Rachel had no contact information for anyone from her past, and she admitted to having amnesia, which made her doubt her own name.

    Last winter came early. We visited Rachel often, and we brought her warm food and drinks. Our relationship grew, but we knew what she really needed was shelter. When the temperature dropped into the teens, we brought Rachel extra blankets and a grilled cheese sandwich that she started eating the second it was in her hands. There were bunk beds in my room, and we decided to give the extra bed to Rachel on a particularly cold night. I was excited at how radical our ministry had become, but this excitement was checked the first night we shared a room. Rachel's clothes smelled so bad from living on the streets that I had to breathe through the blanket. She also had a very loud cough, which kept her (and me) awake at night. When I asked about the cough, she said it was normal.

We decided to invite Rachel to stay with us until our Christmas vacation. She came to Mass with us and participated in Morning Prayer. During the Simple House Christmas breakfast, she feasted and opened presents with us. On our way out of town, though, we drove her back to the soup kitchen and left her out in the cold.

In January, we converted the downstairs living room into a bedroom and invited Rachel to stay with us. I had my room to myself again, but everyone still had to adjust to living together. Rachel was used to being homeless, and she had some habits that were difficult to get used to. She would sleep for only a few hours at a time and be awake at odd hours. She smoked a lot and didn't bathe very often. She insisted on doing the dishes to help out, but she would often leave a lot undone because it was hard for her to stand. She also talked to herself, and these conversations were sometimes quite loud.

We got used to living together as time passed. Rachel spent a lot of time reading, and she adopted our new puppy, Bella. She loved Bella very much. She made sure Bella had food and water, and she slept with Bella during the winter. During this time, we tried to help Rachel get social services, but she had no identification. Until we could get identifying paperwork, there was nothing we could do. Sometimes I would get annoyed at Rachel and become frustrated with our work. I thought, "Where is this going? Is this really doing any good?"

One day in spring, Rachel and a volunteer tried for the third time to get her birth certificate. This time, she remembered the information! Surprisingly, Rachel seemed indifferent to the success. She found her birth certificate in the mail, but she didn't tell us about it until we asked if it had gotten lost. Once she had her birth certificate, we helped her get a nondriver ID. We also helped fill out paperwork for a social security card, food stamps, and Medicare. When her food stamps arrived, Rachel felt like she was rich. She bought food for herself and wanted to share it with everyone. When her Medicare arrived, we got her a doctor's appointment. The doctor was kind and very serious about improving Rachel's health. Rachel went through a bunch of tests, and she started taking blood pressure medicine. Each time we passed a new hurdle, Rachel would tell us that everything wouldn't be this easy. She thought it might all fall apart. I think that's why she didn't react very much to each success; she is used to being disappointed. She has hardened herself against both failure and success.

    We recently discovered that Rachel had been receiving disability checks for over 20 years. She and the representative payee had lost contact when Rachel became homeless. We finally found and contacted the representative payee on Facebook, and she started sending Rachel checks. When the first check was cashed, Rachel disappeared. She hadn't left the house alone in five months, and we were afraid she had returned to the streets. A few hours later, Rachel returned with a shopping bag containing dishrags and coffee mugs. She had walked to the dollar store. She said all our mugs were chipped, and she really liked the rooster design on the mugs she bought. She got the dishrags to protect the mugs in the shopping bag and because we use too many paper towels.

    Rachel didn't seem to have any hopes for herself when she came to live with us. I hoped she would have a place to sleep and get some medical attention, but I couldn't imagine more blessings. Small breakthroughs were always overshadowed by the feeling that there were more problems that needed to be fixed. We never reached a point where we thought we could relax and celebrate our accomplishments. Things happened slowly and not according to our schedule or plans. Even the event that got everything started, Rachel remembering details of her past, didn't come through our work. It simply happened, after a time of persistence.

Looking back on the year, I realize many good things have happened, and Rachel is in a much different place than she was a year ago. She now laughs, makes jokes, and talks about the future. Rachel never went to shelters because of her mental illness, but she was able to come to Simple House because it is a family environment. Thank you for your prayers and support that make this work possible!

God provides for all of us in ways that are often unexpected. He gives us much more than we can imagine for ourselves. Even when we don't notice it, His superabundant providence is a constant sign of the depth of His love for us.

Peace and love,

Danielle Howard

PATRICIA'S BLIZZARD

Dear Friends and Family,   Christmas 2010

    I first met Patricia two years ago when Clark and I brought her home from the hospital. She had been repeatedly abused while growing up, and we were picking her up after an attempt at suicide. She is a sweet and sensitive girl, and through this desperate action, she was crying out for acceptance and love.

    In the past year, Patricia graduated high school and was accepted to college. Throughout the year, Patricia and I grew in friendship as we spent time baking cookies, going to the zoo, and visiting museums in DC. It was exciting helping her through parts of the college enrollment process and planning to drive her to New York for freshmen orientation. She is one of the only people helped by our ministry who has been accepted to college. Her registration and financial aid paperwork were in order and everything was set for her to go to college in the fall of 2010.

    Despite all of the outward success, Patricia faced many interior struggles. Her family has been harsh and unsupportive. She often feels rejected by them. After an argument with her mom, Patricia was kicked out of the house during the DC blizzard.[5] She moved in with a friend, and a few weeks later, she moved back to her mom's house. We climbed over mounds of snow to move trash bags full of her belongings across town.

    Many of Patricia's family members do not know what to do with her. She tries hard to do the right thing,

---

[5] The blizzard of 2010 was the largest two-day snowfall in DC history.

but she is often misunderstood and treated as the "black sheep" of the family. Just two months before moving to college, she was kicked out of the house for a second time. She moved in with her boyfriend and became pregnant. Her mom had pity on her and allowed her to move back in, yet the situation did not get much better. Her mom's friends often stay at the house making it a chaotic and confusing environment. Patricia has also found it difficult to get along with her other siblings.

The expectation of a baby has been a joyful but difficult time for Patricia. She does not have a job or money saved to support her child, and the idea of attending college is fading. At times, Patricia contemplates moving into a shelter because she feels as if she has nowhere else to go.

I am thankful that I can be Patricia's friend during this challenging time. I have repeatedly wondered if I am saying the right thing or helping her in the best way. Not being able to fix Patricia's problems has helped me to realize an important truth: we already have a Savior, and I am not Him.

It is tempting to think, "if I only work hard enough and discover the right solution, I can always fix a situation or person's problem." In reality, the solution lies in lovingly doing what I can and letting God do the rest. There is great freedom in realizing that I cannot fix every problem. I can always offer a caring presence and prayers even when there is no obvious solution. God is the agent of real change and the source of all solutions.

Patricia needs real friendship and material help. Patricia's baby is due in February, and we want to make sure she gets the things she needs to be a good mom and work towards the future. Patricia is still looking for ways to escape the cycle of poverty. She wants to attend college, get a good job, and provide her baby with a loving home. She needs encouragement, support, and prayers. We hope this Christmas will be a time when she will discover God's abundant love for her.

    Many young women face struggles similar to Patricia. Moms often call to ask for diapers and food. It has been a great joy to be welcomed into a mom's exciting and challenging moments. I recently brought one large family some toys and baby clothes which were donated to us. The young mom was thankful for the gift and joked, "Today's like Christmas."
    I am still surprised and humbled when a mom calls and insists that we come to her child's birthday party or a family gathering. We are often treated both as honored guests and part of the family. This is a testament to the growth of a true friendship.
    A Simple House runs a food pantry and mothers' closet to help the poor. In addition, we do many small and unique things to help families through difficult times. All of this help is done with the spirit of friendship and made possible by the generosity of our donors and volunteers. We hope this friendship leads to a transforming relationship with Jesus Christ.

Thank you for your prayers and support.

May God bless you!

Bianca Tropeano

RYAN AND LAURA'S WEDDING

Dear Friends and Family,   Lent 2011

Ryan and Laura are married!

Laura has been involved with A Simple House since the mission was first discerned in 2003. During that first year, we talked about the need for a simple, personal, and rubber-meets-the-road ministry. It would be a Christian support for families in the projects and a place of spiritual growth for volunteers. Laura was the sounding board and discerning guide for these ideas. She was only 19 when she became chairman of the board of A Simple House. Her qualifications were her faith and an intuitive understanding of the ministry.

During the first years of A Simple House, Laura was in college. She volunteered and organized volunteers almost every week. Nine months after her graduation, she became the first resident of the Simple House of the Three Teresas. We did not plan for her to stay long, but someone was needed to house-sit the new house. Five years later, she is still with the ministry.

Laura has the gift of discernment. Despite the risk and strangeness of some ideas, she never dismisses them under the vague pretense of "reasonableness." She is always daring and wise instead of overly conservative or foolhardy.

Laura also has the gift of looking for good and interesting points in people whom others find loathsome, irksome, or just boring. She often says, "I met someone who was kind of being a jerk, but they are interesting because . . ." or "I really like so and so. Despite [insert obvious negative], they are fascinating and good because . . ." She really believes that all men are created in "the image and likeness" of God (Gn 1:26), and an obvious implication is that all people can be appreciated. She even introduced me to my fiancée, Audrey O'Herron.

    After Ryan graduated college, he went to Phoenix, AZ, to serve the homeless for a summer. When he moved back to DC, he seemed like the perfect recruit for A Simple House. I took him out to a $5 pizza buffet and told him that he should join. After a few weeks of discernment, he did.

    Ryan has been at A Simple House for over four years, and he continues to grow in love. There have been at least three turning points in his service. The first one could be called the "mosquitoes have eaten my ankles" conversion. Ryan had been suffering through the bugs, heat, and annoyance of a summer at A Simple house. Summers are the hazing period of voluntary poverty.[6] It is during this time that someone has to tap into the beauty and logic of Christian asceticism or just suffer. Ryan's sacrifices were interfering with his training for a triathlon, and it was wearing down his morale. He turned the corner when he decided to let Christ make these burdens light. He found deeper purpose in his sacrifices, and he even sacrificed some of his ambitions (like the triathlon) in order to serve more.

    About eight months later, he had the "Jesus is the bull's-eye" realization. No ideology (not environmentalism, conservatism, or even pacifism) is fully aligned with Christianity. No matter how close the ideology is to Christ, it is not the bull's-eye that is Christ. We cannot recruit Christ to our ideology. We need to be converted to Christ. This orientation changes everything. Instead of reading our preferences into religion, the

---

[6] See Ryan's letter "Voluntary Poverty" for more details.

religion starts to form our preferences, and Christ really becomes our teacher and head.

Perhaps the greatest turning point was when Ryan started making great sacrifices to rise early in the morning for meditation, prayer, and scripture reading. He even does this after late nights of service, and it made him a coffee drinker. He is able to serve more and pray more than almost anyone I have ever met. His service and prayer do not trade off with one another. They motivate and help one another. The families we serve praise Ryan. They know he makes daily sacrifices for them.

Ryan and Laura were left in charge of the DC houses when I started A Simple House in Kansas City. This made them grow in their gifts of ministry and stewardship. They became responsible for the community, ministry, and finances of the DC houses. They handled stress with a spirit of perseverance and joy. Ryan also learned how to do satirical impressions of me for the entertainment of volunteers. Ryan and Laura plan on staying at A Simple House, and they can because of the generosity of their friends and family.

- Kelly Pertee is a longtime missionary with A Simple House. Her family suffered a tragic loss in January. Her mother and nephew died in a car accident. She is now with her family helping to deal with the tragedy. Her saddened yet beautiful faith has been edifying and comforting to everyone. Please pray for her and her family.

- There is a small Catholic community that meets in a crypt church on the campus of Georgetown University. They have been a huge encouragement and blessing to A Simple House since 2004. For the last few years, this community was led by Fr. John Martin, SJ, who welcomed our begging once a month. In February, Fr. Martin passed away, and this wonderful sub-parish will be closed after Palm Sunday. Please say a special prayer of thanksgiving for Fr. Martin and the parishioners of Copley Crypt.

Thank you for making all of this possible.

Clark Massey

EASTER STORIES

Dear Friends and Family,   Easter 2011

    I met Reina in December 2008. She was struggling financially and expecting her fourth child. We offered to help Reina by getting Christmas gifts for her children and bringing her baby supplies. It was wonderful to deliver the gifts because she was so happy and thankful. She even cried because of her excitement and relief. Her baby was born on Christmas day, and Reina was joyful despite her troubles.

    When I interacted with her over the next year, she was often drunk or high. For the following Christmas, she called at one o'clock at night several nights in a row pleading us to get a Nintendo for her son. I told her no because I was afraid she would pawn it for drugs. My father and I delivered a few gifts to her family on Christmas Eve. She was drunk when we arrived.

    Six months ago, Reina called and said she needed help. She told me she loved her kids, but she was on a path of destruction instead of being a mom. Reina had hit rock bottom, and she didn't even have the clothes and hygiene items to enter drug detoxification. We were honored that Reina called us, and we were excited to help. She entered a three-month drug rehabilitation program the following week.

    Reina is now out of rehab and sober! Though the temptation to smoke crack and PCP remains, this experience has reoriented her life. She is avoiding the people who have tempted her in the past, and she is working hard to comply with court requirements in order to regain custody of her children. The court ordered a parenting class, and she loved it so much she wants to take it again. When asked what she learned, Reina said, "Hollering and cussing at your kids is only going to make them cuss and fuss at each other." Then she emphasized, "I thought I was the perfect parent, and I'm not." In her apartment, Reina has scribbled the names of her kids over and over on a toy chalkboard. Below the names, she has written the Serenity Prayer.

Last Sunday, we brought her and her children to the park for a cookout. This was the first time she had seen them all week, and they were happy for the reunion. It is obvious that Reina's children love her, and her healing is making their lives better.

Reina often goes back and forth between frustration with God and thankfulness to Him. She asks us questions like, "Is it okay to be mad at God?" and "Is God doing this to me, or is this my fault?" She also has to fight loneliness. Since many of Reina's friends enable drug use, we are in a small group who can support her in sobriety. We would not be able to support her without the help of donors. Thank you, and please pray that she will continue to persevere and recover.

Volunteers have been close to Malcolm's family for the last seven years. For much of this time, Malcolm has been in prison for crimes he committed while running the streets. When he got out of prison, he was an amazing and different person. He started taking care of his kids and stayed away from the streets. Surprisingly, he got a job as a security guard, and he even bought a house. His extended family constantly talked about the great transformation.

A few nights before last Thanksgiving, Malcolm was shot in the face. The shooter was someone from his past. His jaw was shattered, and the bullet is permanently lodged in his spine.

Malcolm was in critical condition for weeks. Even months after the attack, it was uncertain if he would live. After six months of hospitalization, Malcolm is finally home. He is paralyzed from the neck down. This has been an important time for us to provide material aid, prayer, and encouragement for his family.

Going to prison was a life-changing event for Malcolm, and now he is in the midst of another transformation. Malcolm used to be a muscular and intimidating man. He is now skinny and helpless. Malcolm is in his twenties and needs his mom to bathe and feed him. He also relies on a respirator, a heart monitor, and an electric wheelchair.

In the past, Malcolm was reserved, and my interactions with him were always brief. His demeanor has been transformed. God has given Malcolm the grace to be open and good humored during this difficult time. When I visited him after his homecoming, he started chatting right away. He congratulated me on getting married, talked about his son, and told us about the movies he had been watching. My ministry partner and I prayed with Malcolm and told him we looked forward to visiting again.

Malcolm and his family have a difficult road before them. There will be many physical and spiritual challenges. We often spend time with his mom letting her vent, and we help her navigate through her frustrations and confusion. She has needed our help to find resources and manage bills. Even with his good attitude, Malcolm sometimes wonders about the purpose of his life. It will be a challenge for us to encourage Malcolm and affirm the worth of his life.

In different ways, Malcolm and Reina have looked at death this past year. Everyone confronts this crisis, and at this moment, Jesus offers life. This is the mystery of the Cross and Resurrection, and it is the center of the Christian life.

God bless you!
Love,

Laura Hehman

SOLIDARITY

Dear Friends and Family,   Thanksgiving 2011

My first weeks at A Simple House were a crash course in simple living. The routine of silent mornings, daily Mass, and prayer, as well as living without Internet and TV, was far from the life I was used to. Living the simple life in an exciting place like Washington, DC, has set me up for a lot of questions from people I meet: "Wait, you do what?" or "You don't have air conditioning?" I respond, "It's weird, I know."

Our reasons for a life of voluntary poverty are twofold. For one, it enables us to live in solidarity with the poor we serve, allowing us to maintain a real empathy for them. Secondly, this simple life helps us to eliminate distractions so that we can be more directed toward our real mission: to befriend the poor and love them as Christ loves them.

Life without constant Internet and TV has led me into deeper prayer. It's amazing how much time there is to read, pray, and reflect when you're bored at home with nothing to entertain you. It's also amazing how clearly God can speak through silence. While I still miss the Food Network and continuous Facebook streams, I've learned to see the beauty in silence, and how little I really need.

I first met Carrie a few weeks ago when Ryan and I were delivering school supplies to families. Carrie is a mentally disabled woman in her mid-thirties, but when I first met her, I didn't think she was much older than her twelve-year-old son, Tyrone. She lives with Tyrone and her mother, Laurie, in a rough project neighborhood. Laurie doesn't allow Carrie to play outside anymore, for good reason.

Years ago, Carrie was taken advantage of in her own neighborhood, resulting in the birth of her only child, Tyrone. Since then, Laurie has become very protective of Carrie, keeping her close at all times. As a result, Carrie spends most of her time inside where her mother, a gruff woman, is very hard on her.

When Ryan and I arrived at the house, Carrie was visibly upset. As we entered, Carrie immediately ran to Ryan for comfort, as a child would seek out a parent. She cried on Ryan's shoulder for a few minutes until Ryan suggested we sit down and talk. "She's been crying like this all day! Won't stop!" Laurie called to us from the other room. Carrie began to explain how she was feeling very sad. After talking for a few minutes, it was very clear that Carrie was incredibly lonely and just wanted someone to talk to. She just wanted to be *loved*.

Ryan took the crucifix from around his neck and handed it to Carrie. He asked, "Do you know who this is?" Carrie looked a little hesitant, but then said that it was Jesus. Ryan told Carrie that Jesus loves her very much and He would always listen to her prayers. She took the crucifix from Ryan and clutched it to her cheek as she began to pray the most innocent and childlike of prayers. "I love you Jesus, will you listen to me? I *know* you will listen to me." Then she kissed the cross and placed it around her neck. It was an incredible gift to witness such beautiful childlike faith.

We made plans with Laurie to take Carrie to the zoo the following week in order to get her out of the house and give her some much-needed attention. When we arrived at Carrie's house, she was eagerly waiting for us in the parking lot. As she got in the car, I noticed

Carrie was wearing the crucifix Ryan had given her. "We match!" she said, smiling.

We had a great time with Carrie at the zoo. We spent extra time with her favorite animal, the lion, and took a break for cherry snow cones before heading home. As we dropped her off, I couldn't help but think that she was simply going back into the chaos she has grown up in, and that nothing would really change in her life. What's the point? The point is Christ loves Carrie more than any of us ever could, and we're called to show her that.

> We can cure physical diseases with medicine, but the only cure for loneliness, despair, and hopelessness is love. There are many in the world who are dying for a piece of bread, but there are many more dying for a little love.
>
> -Bl. Teresa of Calcutta

Love and friendship are real needs among the poor. Mother Teresa saw this and made it her entire mission to minister to those who were forgotten and unloved. Even when the poor have their material needs met, there still exists despair and hopelessness. This can lead to problems such as violent crime, a culture without long-term goals, and the lack of will to maintain the few possessions they have. We can give a man something to eat, but if he does not know love, what does he have? "Man does not live on bread alone" (Mt 4:4).

We call our method of helping the poor "friendship evangelization." We aim to befriend the poor and minister to their individual needs as Jesus would. For some, our friendship involves guiding them in moral teaching, studying scripture, and even taking them to Mass. For others, ministry means bringing groceries to feed their family and joining hands in prayer before we leave. For Carrie, her need was to be given attention and introduced to the love of Christ in a tangible way.

I humbly ask that you help me in the mission of A Simple House in whatever way you can. For some, that may mean supporting us financially; for others, it may be a commitment to prayer for our ministry and its continued growth. If you are able to give financially, please consider becoming a monthly donor instead of giving a onetime gift. Money can be tight during the year, so having that monthly commitment is very helpful. I thank you in advance for whatever you can give. It is solely people like you who keep our doors open each month.

Know that you are in my prayers!

In Christ,

Mary Manion

NETWORKING

Dear Friends and Family,   Christmas 2011

    Melissa was let out of a pickup truck outside a homeless soup kitchen. To her surprise, the pickup drove away and abandoned her. Melissa is pregnant, mentally ill, and now homeless. She often talks to herself and is confused about her past and current situation. Our homeless friend David saw how she was abandoned, and he explained how the soup line works. Although David has shown her the ropes of living on the street, Melissa has a curious inability to help herself.

    Melissa stays in a homeless camp all day talking to herself, and she always appears to be in some physical pain. Because she will not go to the soup lines, David has to "fly a sign" at the edge of the highway, and he uses the money to feed her. He kept up this vigil for weeks as we started a relationship with her. He received nothing in return. It gave him purpose, but it was driving him crazy.

    David usually flew a sign for himself to buy cigarettes and alcohol. Now that he was helping Melissa, it was taking a toll on his smoking and drinking. He kept telling me, "Clark, you really have to do something about this." I told him to hold on because we needed more time to gain her trust. We were working to get her medical attention and shelter. I knew it was good for him to help her out, and when he complained that it hurt his drinking, I started to laugh. He was loving and serious when he told me, "This isn't funny!"

    After communicating with Melissa's family, we bought her a bus ticket to her hometown 600 miles away.

One of our volunteers, Caitrin, is accompanying her on the bus ride. Melissa has not been home in years, and her family is eager to welcome her.

Simple House volunteers have extensively worked with five women who have suffered mental illness and homelessness. It appears that their illness caused their homelessness. David brought two of these women to A Simple House for help.

David has a cell phone, and he calls us when he meets someone on the streets who "should not be there." The first call came about a year and a half ago. It was raining, and he was sitting underneath a bridge with a twenty-year-old woman who would barely speak. I walked to the bridge, and she wouldn't talk to me when I got there. I gave her our information, and over the next few weeks, we started a relationship with her over pizza and burgers.

During Thanksgiving 2010, the head of our Kansas City house invited her to move into A Simple House. Although she was not willing at first, her trust grew, and she agreed to move in. She spent most of the time trying to work on herself and sort out her thoughts without the help of a doctor. She had a mental breakdown in May, and the situation became so bad that we had to ask her to leave. Over the next few months, volunteers took her to multiple psychiatric emergency rooms, and she finally received quality help. Due to the persistence of Simple House volunteers and hospital staff, she now has an apartment and long-term mental health support. Although the process was very stressful, it seems miraculous how much things have improved.

Her family recently visited Kansas City, and they helped her set up the apartment. They had not kicked her out or given up on her, but a person may choose homelessness due to paranoia or because they don't want psychiatric help. At that point, the family is usually confused and completely drained. In many cases, the person leaves their hometown and loses contact with their family. It is necessary for a loving and trustworthy outsider to become involved and help the person become open to help.

There are people who fall into temporary homelessness due to misfortune or bad choices. These people are some of the easiest to help, and there are many programs to help them find housing. Persistent homelessness is usually caused by drug addiction, alcoholism, or mental illness. Love is the precursor and companion to useful psychiatric and material help. People need to know that they are accepted with their problems before they allow someone to share their struggles.

It is a missionary's job to make the love of Christ credible. A gentle loving witness erodes away distrust, and it can enable someone to address the reality of their situation. As for the five homeless and mentally ill women we have served, Melissa is returning to her family, one was given housing by another organization, and A Simple House has sheltered three of them until they received more permanent housing. Your generosity makes this possible.

A Simple House serves the poorest of the poor with material aid and love. Our work is focused on families living in Section 8 and project housing, but homeless ministry has always been a part of A Simple House too. During December, the Kansas City house will start a weekly homeless outreach. We are able to do this because of the help of many donors and fervent volunteers. We are also able to do this because of David.

He keeps us informed, and he has a great enthusiasm for helping his fellow homeless.

- Two seminarians from Denver will serve the poor and live at A Simple House in Kansas City for the month of January. They are sent in twos to serve the poor. In addition, there are three seminarians currently serving as part-time volunteers: Adam from the Amarillo Diocese; Clay from the Wichita Diocese; and Br. Al of the Capuchin Franciscans.

- A family has asked to be baptized and enter the Church on Easter. Volunteers first met the family during an Easter outreach.

Thank you for always supporting this work.

Clark Massey

A TURTLE AND A CHICKEN

Dear Friends and Family, Lent 2012

    Danny's family is one of the poorest families we have ever met. He lives with his elderly mother and his brother. When we met them last October, their gas and electricity had been off for six months. They live in a big apartment complex in the inner city, but they are basically camping. They owe thousands of dollars on overdue bills, and any financial help we could give them would only be a drop in the bucket.

    Throughout the winter, we have tried to meet their immediate bodily needs with blankets and food. We brought them a tray of baked chicken, and they stopped eating it only after it went bad and made them sick. They cook over Sterno, so we brought them cans of soup from the food pantry. When the fuel runs out, they eat the soup cold straight from the can or just fill up on peanut butter and jelly sandwiches.

    They have no way to do laundry, so dirty clothes pile up in mounds around the apartment. "We wear our clothes over and over and over, and that is so depressing," Danny's mother told me, almost in tears. We washed a few loads of laundry for her at our house, but many piles remain. They also keep a turtle and a live chicken in the apartment for entertainment, which doesn't help keep things clean. It is shocking to see how they live, even in the poorest neighborhood of the city.

Danny and his brother struggle with alcoholism. Any money they could have spent on bills probably went towards liquor. Danny is in his forties, and he is meek, light hearted, and friendly. Nonetheless, alcohol has made a mess of his life, and he knows it. His father died from health problems related to drinking, and his own mistakes have estranged him from his teenage daughter. The first time we met Danny, he asked us to pray that God would free him from alcoholism. On another occasion, he broke down sobbing, repenting, and begging for help with his addiction.

Twice he tried to admit himself into the detox program at a nearby hospital. Each time, he got scared and left before they could admit him. When we found this out, we made arrangements to take him to detox and sit with him until he was admitted.

I arrived at Danny's house at 10:30 am, but he was already at the liquor store begging for change so he could buy his first drink. Earlier that morning, his mother reminded him about detox, but he brushed her off and said he had changed his mind. We drove to the liquor store and arrived just in time to see him kill the last of a bottle. As we pulled up, I asked God for help and wondered if this was a good idea.

To my surprise, Danny was happy to see us. He got into the car, and we bought him a McDonald's hamburger and a change of clothes that he could bring to detox. Then we went to the hospital and waited with him all day until he was admitted.

Danny and I knew that detox wouldn't solve all his problems, but it was an important first step. He knew what he had to do—and wanted to do—but he lacked the confidence and encouragement to go through with it.

He stayed at the hospital for a week, and it was much easier than he expected. The tough part was going home. To get there, Danny had to walk past the liquor store and all the familiar faces. At home he has to deal with his brother and friends, who still regularly get drunk and carry on in his living room. Without gas or electricity, the whole family has to deal with boredom and discomfort from the cold. In such a discouraging environment, it is easy to turn back to drinking.

As of this letter, Danny is six weeks sober, and it is a miracle! We've helped him find the nearest AA meetings, and he attends them regularly. He also left the city for a week to stay with his sister and clear his mind. His progress is amazing, and your generosity ensures that we can continue supporting Danny.

A few weeks ago, Danny was a bum on the street corner begging for change. Meeting a bum on the street corner is a difficult encounter for everyone. We are hesitant to give money because we are concerned that it will add to his problems, not fix them. We are sometimes right. When we conclude that his predicament is his own fault and therefore he doesn't deserve our help, we are wrong. Jesus came for sinners, not for the righteous (Mk 2:17). Everybody can be redeemed, and nobody is too lost to be loved.

The real issue is not whether to give money. No one's life is made or broken by a dollar. A better question is how can I respond with love to someone in need? The poorest people are most in need of an investment of time and friendship. Not everyone is in a position to make this investment, but we are all called to do what we can.

At A Simple House, we are trying to invest time, resources, and love into the families who are most in need. Sometimes this includes supporting single mothers, giving Christmas gifts to children, visiting the elderly, or encouraging someone to make a loving choice. Whatever the situation, your gifts help us to meet the needs of the poor with personal attention.

In Christ,

Ryan Hehman

THE WOODSMAN

Dear Friends and Family,   Easter 2012

    The Missouri and Kansas rivers meet in downtown Kansas City. The skyline sits on a bluff above the rivers, and below the bluff is a railroad hub second only to Chicago in capacity and size. The railroads, casinos, and warehouses that are built in this floodplain are protected by a two-story-high levee.

    Between the levee and the river is a no-man's-land. It is a two-hundred-yard forested area running along the river, and it is the first area to flood when the river rises. Unlike railroad or city land, it is unclear who has authority over this land, and it is a campground for dozens of homeless people.

    Tyler is the "mayor" of one of these homeless settlements. Tyler lives in an eight-sided cabin that resembles a yurt. It has a skylight and wood-burning stove. It is made with leftover deck materials, tarpaper, two-by-fours, and plastic sheeting. Watermarks are halfway up the walls from last year's flood. Tyler has lived here for ten years.

    There are three tents of people living near Tyler, and he built a heated booth nearby to help fellow sojourners find shelter. Tyler is a hospitable and welcoming face in the floodplain. The settlement is a fascinating accomplishment and a sadness simultaneously.

    There are women and men in the homeless camps, and the residents range from 18 to 60 years old. In

Tyler's opinion, confirmed by our experience, there are three reasons for this type of desperate homelessness: addiction, running from the law, and mental illness. Financial misfortune and bad luck are not enough to bring someone to the river.

Addiction can consume every dime of a person's income. People can start to prefer the "freedom" of the camp and the frequent drinking parties to the responsibilities and stress of normal society. The Honor Center is located in the river bottoms, and the Department of Corrections sends people there on work release. If they violate the terms of parole, they may choose to live in the woods rather than go back to a higher security prison. In addition, there are mentally ill people who refuse treatment but cannot integrate into society enough to find employment or shelter.

As if it were a rule, the drug addicts and the alcoholics are the ones begging for money. Frequently, someone will receive $50 or more while begging on a corner and none of it will be saved for the next day. The homeless who only struggle with mental illness do not beg.

Tyler had some interesting ideas about how spirituality and psychology need to be integrated. He also seemed like a great person to help us understand how to best serve the homeless. We usually meet at A Simple House on Tuesdays to discuss a theological article, but on one Tuesday afternoon, Kansas City missionaries went to the river and met with Tyler.

This meeting was informative in many ways. We heard some interesting thoughts on psychology, but we also learned that Tyler had not visited his family for twenty years. He occasionally calls, but he had not seen them since leaving prison in 1992. They live about four hours away, and he has three grandchildren he has never met.

Tyler does small odd jobs for money, and he does not beg. People in the camp keep him supplied with beer because of the help he provides everyone. I asked Tyler if he were given an income (such as disability or social security) would he rent an apartment. He said no. He is a woodsman and prefers the woods. His impressive camping skills make that claim believable. He even livetraps raccoons with a baited shopping cart.

Ashley asked him where he buys food in the railroad district. He said that he never buys food. There are so many agencies and generous strangers providing food there is no need to spend money on it. As we ended the meeting, I asked how someone in the camp would spend a ten-dollar bill. He said, "Three dollars would go to cigarettes, and seven dollars would go to beer." I had already decided that we needed to help people leave the camp as opposed to improving the camp. As I heard Tyler talk, I wondered if we should even be helping with food and supplies. I asked Tyler if he thought it was enabling, and he said probably. He said the best way to help is to be a friend. That is what we are trying to do.

My wife and I drove Tyler to spend a few days with his family. Please pray that renewing these family relationships will motivate him to move back home. Thank you for making this work possible.

Your generosity has also helped Mark. He is a bookworm who lived in the camp, but he stayed away from all of the drugs and alcohol. Although Mark is shy, we slowly got to know him over shared meals. He found a kitchen job through a church friend. Your generosity rented a motel room for him while he began working and helped Mark rent an apartment after he received a complete paycheck. He has been away from the river for about two months, and we pray that his success continues.

God is Generous

- We sold our house in Northwest Washington, DC. It sold after only 7 days on the market. We want to buy a more suitable property in Southeast DC. Everyone will be crowded into our house on Minnesota Ave in Southeast DC until the new property is bought. Please pray for our continued growth in DC.

- Joseph Hehman was born to Laura and Ryan on February 28. Congrats to our longtime volunteers becoming parents!

- A family was baptized and joined the Church this Easter. Please pray for their continued conversion and grace. We first met them during an outreach two years ago, and it has been a blessing to know them during their conversion.

Thank you and please keep us in your prayers!

Clark Massey

Mark's Story

Dear Friends and Family,   Thanksgiving 2012

    Two years ago, Mark was shot. The incident left him paralyzed from the neck down. Tragically, the shooting was right after Mark began to turn his life around. Living the street life, he had been caught up with misguided people and the wrong influences from a young age. With an entirely new set of challenges, Mark must overcome more than just his past.

    Taking care of Mark is a big responsibility. It requires special medical equipment, extra expenses, and a lot of time. A few months ago his mother, overwhelmed from the burden, sent him to stay at a hospital. When I walked into Mark's hospital room, he was choking on fluids stuck in his throat. He had pushed the call button, but nobody came to help him! Mark rarely has any visitors at all, not even family members. It is clear that he is not bathed regularly, and his caretakers pretty much ignore him. In the same room, day after day, Mark lies alone in a hospital bed, surrounded by blank walls. He said, "I feel like I am in prison." Before he was shot, Mark spent time in jail, so he would know. Yet, Mark has not given up hope. Through this immense suffering and lonely confinement, he remains open and loving. He is not bitter, even though he has many reasons to be. He spends his time thinking and praying, and he is very excited to learn about Jesus and read from the Bible. We planned on spending a few minutes with Mark, but those minutes quickly turned into an hour.

Mother Teresa said "Being unwanted, unloved, uncared for, forgotten by everybody, I think that is a much greater hunger, a much greater poverty than the person who has nothing to eat." The world doesn't want Mark. He is weak, unable to move or accomplish anything by himself. A Simple House can be a friend to Mark by helping him with daily tasks: readjusting pillows, drinking water, making phone calls. Besides physical assistance, we can address the spiritual poverty of which Mother Teresa speaks by spending time with Mark and encouraging his hope.

Kendra has eight children. She is battling depression, and her children often add to her stress by making her household chaotic. Mark's life lacks company; Kendra's life lacks quiet. Kendra has been attending a program to help her with her depression. To aid Kendra, we have started an after school ministry with her family, and I've begun to lead her youngest kids in Bible studies. When first teaching the girls about God, they were especially eager to point out God's creation. At the park, the two five-year-old twins pointed out everything God made, including the clouds, the flowers, and even a rainbow. We made up a chant to sing in the car ride home about everything God made. They were so excited to find out that "God made *everyone*?" "Yes, everyone!" "Even the people all the way over in China?" I couldn't help but chuckle. Teaching the girls that each person has been made in the image of God reminded me that our dignity comes from being children of the Creator.

A day after meeting Mark, I found out that he is my age. Still on the heels of my graduation from William & Mary, my life seems different from Mark's. He is paralyzed, has been to jail, and has three children. Likewise, Kendra's children experience different surroundings than I did in my childhood. I didn't grow up in a rough neighborhood like Kendra's family, where gunshots could be heard outside the door at night. I wonder how I can relate. Still, we share a crucial similarity. This similarity runs deeper than differences that appear to separate us, like our family background, race, and education. We are children of God. This shared humanity is the similarity that binds us closely to every other person despite differences. Each of us is just like Mark, or Kendra, or her kids. We all struggle each day and search to be wanted and loved by somebody. Intimately witnessing the struggles of others has caused me to reflect on my own sorrow resulting from the death of my biggest brother, Ben, this past summer. Our pains, circumstances, and temptations vary, but our hope can be the same. In every significant way, I am not different from anyone else in Southeast DC. We are all alike. We are children of God, loved by Love Himself. "God is love" (1 Jn 4:8). Even if Mark's life appears to be purposeless, his life—like Kendra's, her children, and the rest of ours—can be fulfilled through loving the Lord and hoping for the Kingdom to come.

My efforts at A Simple House are encouraged by this anticipation of Heaven, eventually being united to God and my brother. A Simple House's book club is reading the *Compendium of the Social Doctrine of the Church.* The compendium explains anticipation for eternal life: "This hope, rather than weaken, must instead strengthen concern for the work that is needed in the present reality." There is much work to be completed in Southeast DC, many friendships to be fortified. There are more people to visit, to bring groceries to, to pray with, to give hope to.

Peace and Love,
Liz Horne

Victims or Losers

Dear Friends and Family,　　　　　Christmas 2012

　　Are the poor victims or losers? Should we only give to people ready to succeed, or serve people even when nothing seems to work? I have shared many ministry stories with my friends and family. Some of the stories are inspiring and some are tragic. Many people, including myself, struggle with a polar view of the poor.

　　Everyone is made in the image and likeness of God, so everyone should be likable. Simple House volunteers befriend the abused and downtrodden. We also befriend murderers, felons, negligent parents, prostitutes, and abusers. It is easy to ruin friendships by feeling disdain because of someone's "unworthiness" or dysfunction. That type of judgment is what Jesus forbids. We need to make practical judgments and use spiritual insight about the probable success of ministry, but should we still serve people even when there is not much hope for success?

　　I have been working with many homeless people living on the Missouri river. Some want to change and others don't. Jim and Kate are an example of two people who want to change. They left the river and now stay at A Simple House. They are both working, and they should be in their own apartment before Christmas. Jim and Kate are a very satisfying and successful part of our ministry. Jim even cooked a Thanksgiving dinner for the Simple House volunteers. Thank you for giving us the opportunity and financial resources to help them get back on their feet.

Mike and Joe are two more friends from the river. In August, we took Mike and Joe to a free health clinic, and when we picked them up, we invited them to daily Mass. They accepted, and we worshipped in a very small congregation with our parish priest Fr. Ernie. They talked to Fr. Ernie and agreed to talk more about the faith in the future. Joe was murdered three days later. Mike reported the murder, and he is being held as the primary suspect. I visit Mike once a week and send him books in the county jail. Please pray for both of them. Joe's photo is included.

There is something deeply worthwhile about life even when life looks like a failure. At certain graced moments, I feel the privilege of seeing people almost as God sees them. At these moments, everyone becomes so interesting. People are not just holy or lovable; they are interesting and likable. Every life seems like a book with an incredibly complex story. The world would be poorer if William Shakespeare had not written tragedies. Even more so, there would be a cosmic spiritual loss if even one person did not exist.

The poor are part of humanity's treasure. It is not good to ignore them or wish them away. Instead of seeing value in a person's achievements or gifts, life has a more basic and intrinsic value. God intended everyone, and His intention is special. Although it seems painful and crazy at times, God is working a beautiful and amazing plan in humanity.

I told Mike about this idea during a visit. I was not trying to encourage him or point a finger at him. It was a burning idea, and it needed to be aired with someone. Mike had just finished a book he found on the jail book cart by Viktor Frankl. Frankl survived a Nazi concentration camp, and he tackles one of the ultimate questions: Why does life have value in the face of pain, guilt, and death? He argues for a tragic optimism. In Christianity, life has value, hope, and true optimism. As missionaries, we need to help people feel their intrinsic worth in the midst of tragedy. We need to make this more than a "theoretical" or "faith alone" value. It needs to be a buoy for existence.

Jesus serves people who never seem to succeed, and He wants us to serve them too. Loving the seemingly unlovable images God, and it gives witness by loving with no perceptible return.

Simple House is moving in DC and opening an additional house. The new house will be A Simple House of St. Jude. St. Jude is one of the 12 apostles, cousin of Jesus, and patron saint of hopeless causes. I hope his patronage will keep volunteers encouraged while serving everyone.

What is Evangelization?

Being without God is the worst type of disability. Evangelization is reaching out to people who are suffering. It may not end in a baptism, but it must always end in giving someone a greater closeness and experience of God. When we view evangelization as a partisan activity, we are not helping anyone, and we hurt ourselves.

Important Note: The Thanksgiving letter told Mark's story. After Mark turned his life around a few years ago, he was shot and paralyzed by an old acquaintance. Unexpectedly, Mark passed away after the letter was sent. Mark's disposition and joy were a wonder and inspiration. Please pray for Mark and his family.

Clark Massey

Pit Bulls and Thanksgiving Turkeys

Dear Friends and Family,   Summer 2013

    As I stood in front of Derrick's house, four pit bulls barked and snarled at me from the yard, which was basically a dirt pit. I had not yet met Derrick, and I didn't anticipate this obstacle when he called asking for Thanksgiving food. I tried calling his house phone, but there was no answer. Then I called out his name from the sidewalk, but there was no sign of life inside. It was the day before Thanksgiving, and if I didn't leave the food, he wouldn't get it. I took a deep breath and cautiously opened the gate to the yard. The barking got louder, but thankfully none of the dogs bit me!

    Derrick eventually came to the door and was genuinely embarrassed by his dogs. He smacked the one sniffing at my feet and quickly shuffled us inside. The house was dark and dirty. Everything was stained. As the smell of dog urine stung my nose, I thought I would have been more comfortable in the yard.

    Derrick was under house arrest for violating a condition of his parole. To prove it, he pointed to a black locator box strapped to his ankle that recorded his whereabouts. Until then, I had only seen them in movies. He normally relied on his girlfriend to run errands, but she left town to visit family. As a result, he couldn't go out to buy any food to celebrate the holiday.

    Our conversation was tense and didn't last long. I asked about his dogs. He kept them mainly because he liked dogs but also for protection (he was living in the most dangerous neighborhood in Southeast DC). Once the conversation died, he reluctantly agreed to pray with us, and we left. I didn't expect to see him again.

I met Derrick in 2007. Since then, he has called almost every month asking for groceries. It took a long time to get to know Derrick through our short visits. Each time we met, we would chat a little and pray that he could find a job. He has grown to like and trust us, and we have learned more about his life.

Derrick is in his late 30s and has been incarcerated on two separate occasions. Towards the end of his last sentence, he was given an unlikely cellmate: his father. Because they have different last names, no one in the prison realized the two were related until they were bunked together. They had not seen each other since Derrick was a boy, and neither one was interested in a reunion. Derrick blamed most of his troubles on his father's absence, and they were soon separated because of their arguing.

Ironically, Derrick's youngest son was born while he was in jail. He met him for the first time three years later on a city bus, when he ran into his old girlfriend. Noticing that the boy looked like him, he asked if it was his son, and the mother reluctantly replied that it was. Years of custody battles and child support hearings followed.

These two experiences deeply troubled Derrick. He worried he was becoming like his father. I met him shortly after they happened, at a very low point in his life. This may partially explain the chaotic and dark environment he was living in.

For a few years, I wondered if we were really helping Derrick and if we were even welcome in his home. At first, he only seemed interested in groceries. But as time went on, a real friendship developed. I invited him to my wedding in 2011, and I was surprised when I spotted him in the back pew. He had not been to church since he was a child.

Then came another surprise. One day, he called me and said, "I wanted to let you know our prayers have been answered. I got a job at Nationals Stadium washing dishes." Hallelujah! I was happy that he found a job, but I was even happier that he said, "Our prayers have been answered."

Derrick has been slowly changing his life. He no longer lives in the house where I met him but in a clean apartment. He no longer keeps dogs. Although he doesn't have a permanent full-time job, he has a steady succession of temporary jobs. I like to call Derrick "the hardest working man in "because he is always hitting the streets applying for jobs, interviewing, and attending job fairs. He is about to get full custody of his three children, a long-awaited event that both excites and scares him. He makes sure we pray together at the end of our visits, and he often tells me how his prayers have been answered.

Receiving answers to prayer has given Derrick hope. He no longer thinks he is doomed to follow his father's path. In his situation, I see an important scriptural promise coming to life: "'For I know the plans I have for you,' says the Lord, 'plans to prosper you and not to harm you, plans to give you hope and a future" (Jer 29:11).

Sometimes people ask me if we see any conversions. I tell them about folks like Derrick, and they seem disappointed. They must mean dramatic "lightning bolt" conversions in which people suddenly give up their evil ways and are changed forever. I see plenty of conversion but very few lightning bolts. Most people are like Derrick – they are fighting through their conversion one day and one decision at a time.

Conversion is hard work! Derrick is extraordinary because he is willing to do the hard work. When we expect people to change overnight, we fail to realize how long it has taken for their problems to develop in the first place. Frequently, it takes a long time to change because many wounds and habits of sin are deeply ingrained. Nonetheless, we are confident that God, who has begun this good work in Derrick, will carry it to completion.

Your generosity enables us to help Derrick. Even when we are only providing small helps, we use these interactions to build meaningful relationships and convey the love of God. Please continue your support of our work in reaching out to families in Washington, DC, and Kansas City.

In Christ,

Ryan Hehman

Grace Abounds

Dear Friends and Family,   Fall 2013

    In June, the police came into the homeless camp we serve and told everyone to move. At the end of the week, the camp was bulldozed. Many of the homeless relocated their tents to other parts of the woods. Phil and Gina had lived in the camp for 6 months, and their friend offered them a trailer. The trailer was barely livable. It had no running water or usable toilet. The floor was broken plywood, and the dirty furniture was left by a former occupant. Despite the horrible environment, Phil and Gina moved in with their few possessions, including two pit bulls and a large crate of canned food. They were excited and wanted to make it a permanent home.

    The water was off because the copper pipes had frozen and burst during a previous winter. We made trips to Home Depot and spent a few days trying to help Phil and Gina fix their water pipes. Each time a leaky pipe was fixed, another was found. This seemed like a ridiculous waste of time; however, it was good to see Phil working with Dave, the dad of one of our missionaries. (He came to KC with his wife to do mission work for a month.) Like many of the homeless, Phil is an alcoholic. It was good to see him working passionately on a project instead of drinking.

    As Dave and Phil worked on the water pipes, I sat on the porch and talked with Gina. Gina is in her forties and mentally handicapped. She also has Tourettes. Phil and Gina are originally from Ohio and met in special needs classes. One afternoon, while enjoying a lunch of

McDonald's burgers and fries, Gina showed me her dogs and told me about her mom and two sons. She asked me to speak on the phone with her mom and son during our visit. I was humbled that she introduced me to them as "her friend."

A few weeks later, Gina called Clark to tell him that Phil had been arrested. In a drunken rage, he murdered his elderly neighbor with a hammer. Clark and I went to visit Gina early the next morning. I was surprised that she was still staying in the trailer across from the crime scene. We spent the morning helping her get food stamps and allowing her to speak about how she was feeling. We ended with plans to help Gina get into a homeless shelter. When we went looking for Gina, we were told she had been admitted to a hospital for a panic attack and entered a witness protection program. A couple of weeks later, Gina called us for a ride. Other than her mom, who lives out of state, we are one of the few people she has to call.

"Where sin abounds, grace abounds all the more" (Rom 5:20). Many people dwell on the first part and not on the second. There are many ministry situations where we see the horror of sin and the effects of people's bad decisions. Many people fall into despair and think we live in tragic times. Yet, I am struck with awe by the way God allows us to see His active and abundant grace in the midst of great wrongdoing.

God has called us to patiently love the poor in simple ways, caring for their specific and individual needs. Sometimes God asks us to let go of situations and allow Him to work. Our friend, Fr. Adam Ryan, OSB, said, "Some things are above our pay grade." There are many things we cannot fix, but we can love in little ways. It is through these consistent little ways of love that God chooses to work great miracles.

Sometimes, we attempt to understand the horror of sin. This is an endless search that leaves us dissatisfied. Although difficult to comprehend, we should conclude: Sin is ugly and God is Mercy. God does not ask us to understand the horrors of sin, he asks that we have hope in his mercy. He asks us to trust that his love is offered to each of us, even to those who commit grave sins. We need more hope, trust, and faith. In many ways, this is a mystery we constantly wrestle with, the mystery of free will and God's Love, freely given.

This August, Jamal and Shawn entered college. They are the first people in their families to go to college. Jamal is from a family we have known in DC for over 9 years. He is one of 8. After working hard with our missionaries, he was accepted to a historically black college in Ohio. Last year, we gave Jamal's mom a van. She drove Jamal to school and moved him onto campus. Jamal does not have a computer, and he works in the library to do his schoolwork. Jamal seems to be doing well, and we hope to continue supporting him.

Shawn is from a family we have known in KC for over 4 years. In many ways it is a miracle that Shawn was accepted to college. When Shawn was a baby, he ate a large amount of lead paint, causing some cognitive damage, which impaired his ability to learn. When Shawn was 6, his father was murdered. Shawn vividly remembers learning on TV that his dad was shot in the chest multiple times and died.

Shawn grew up surrounded by poverty and violence, and he attended the roughest high school in Kansas City. Despite having special needs, Shawn led a weekly bible study at his school during lunch. He was respected among his peers and talked about Jesus so much that he got the nickname "Jesus Kid." He has chosen a path very different from many of his peers.

Even in his home life, Shawn stands out as an exceptional person. His extended family is one of the poorest families we know. The young kids are frequently hungry for food and attention, and the moms move every few months to escape paying bills.

    Shawn wanted to enroll in Bible College to become a pastor, and with some help, he was accepted to a small college in Overland Park, KS. When Shawn left for college, he took two trash bags, a bucket of shoes, and a broken light-up Angel statue, which he said was good luck. We helped him buy some bedding and toiletries to complete his supplies.

    Shawn stayed at college for three weeks. His learning disabilities and lack of preparation made college impossible. College is not for everyone; however, in many ways the Kansas City school system failed Shawn. It allowed him to graduate without the ability to spell the school's name. Shawn's lack of preparation was apparent only after his first few days of class. Shawn is so charismatic and high functioning that we did not realize how much his education was lacking until he got to college. The college tried to accommodate him, but this was not enough. We will help Shawn find a good job and encourage him to continue sharing God's love with his family and community.

Thank you for your support and prayers.

In Christ,

Bianca Tropeano

Although this book is over, these letters are still being written. If you would like to receive future letters, please sign up at: **asimplehouse.org**

- A Simple House qualifies under section 501(c)(3) of the internal revenue code. There is a board of directors that meets quarterly, and the legal name of the nonprofit is "Sts. Francis and Alphonsus." "A Simple House" is a registered trade name.

- A Simple House is an all-volunteer ministry. Full-time volunteers are given a subsistence stipend. The volunteer nature of the ministry helps to ensure that the greatest part of every donation goes to help the poor, and it helps volunteers maintain purity of heart while building the Kingdom.

- A Simple House observes corporate poverty by renouncing endowments and savings accounts. As a general rule, the ministry has less than three months operating expenses at all times. When the ministry receives bountiful donations, these donations are given to the poor. Corporate poverty helps ensure that the greatest part of every donation goes to the poor, and it keeps volunteers praying for the ministry's daily bread.

ORTHODOXY
ORTHOPRAXIS

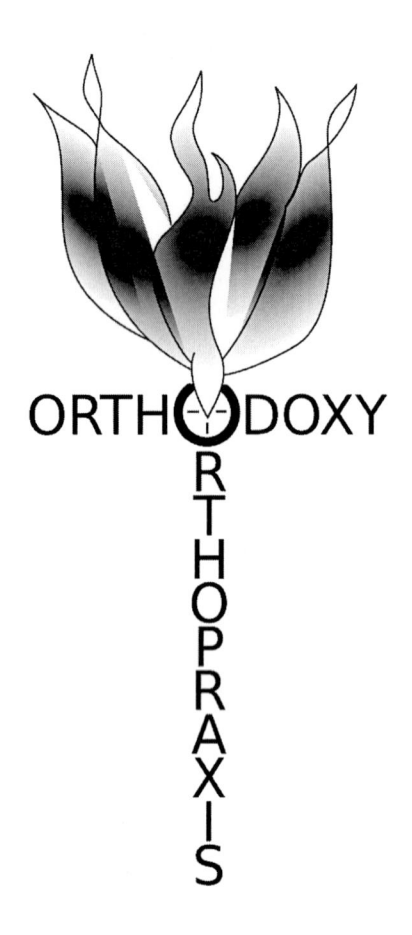

ASimpleHouse.org